The Short Story Series

GENERAL EDITOR   JAMES GIBSON

ADVENTURE
AMERICAN
ANIMAL
COUNTRY
CRIME
DETECTION
FANTASY
HORROR
HUMOUR
LOVE
SCIENCE FICTION
SEA
SPORT
SUPERNATURAL
SUSPENSE
TRAVEL
WAR
WESTERN

The Short Story Series

War

CHOSEN BY
James Gibson

John Murray
Albemarle Street London

Typeset by Inforum Ltd, Portsmouth.
Printed and bound in Great Britain
by Butler and Tanner Ltd,
Frome and London

British Library Cataloguing in Publication Data

War – (The Short story series)
1. Children's stories, English
I. Gibson, James 1919–
823′ .01′089292 [J]   PZ5

ISBN 0-7195-3871-8

Contents

Intelligence   *C. S. Forester*   1

The Young Man from Kalgoorlie   *H. E. Bates*   13

Monsoon Selection Board
   George MacDonald Fraser   24

Turning Point   *Alan Green*   31

Death of the Zulu   *Uys Krige*   40

They Came   *Alun Lewis*   48

The Alien Skull   *Liam O'Flaherty*   60

Wingult   *R. J. Binding*   67

The Miracle   *Walter Duranty*   79

Death of a Cat   *Axel Eggebrecht*   88

The Boy Spy   *Alphonse Daudet*   94

The Affair at Coulter's Notch   *Ambrose Bierce*   101

The Spoils of War   *Carey Blyton*   109

The Last Galley   *Sir Arthur Conan Doyle*   115

Acknowledgements   122

C. S. Forester

Intelligence

Captain George Crowe, C.B., D.S.O., R.N., walked down three short steps into the blinding sunshine that made the big aeroplane's wings seem to waver in reflected light. The heat of the Potomac Valley hit him in the face, a sweltering contrast to the air-cooled comfort of the plane. He was wearing a blue uniform more suitable for the bridge of a destroyer than for the damp heat of Washington, and that was not very surprising, because not a great many hours earlier he had been on the bridge of a destroyer, and most of the intervening hours he had spent in aeroplanes, sitting in miserable discomfort at first, breathing through his oxygen mask in the plane that had brought him across the Atlantic, and then reclining in cushioned ease in the passenger plane that had brought him from his point of landing here.

The United States naval officer who had been sent to meet him had no difficulty in picking him out—the four gold stripes on his sleeves and the ribbons on his chest marked him out, even if his bulk and his purposeful carriage had not done so.

'Captain Crowe?' asked the naval lieutenant.

'Yes.'

'Glad to see you, sir. My name's Harley.'

The two shook hands.

'I have a car waiting, sir,' Harley went on. 'They're expecting you at the Navy Department, if you wouldn't mind coming at once.'

The car swung out of the airport and headed for the bridge while Crowe blinked round him. It was a good deal of a contrast—two days before he had been with his flotilla, refuelling in a home port; then had come the summons to the Admiralty, a fleeting glimpse of wartime London, and now here he was in the District of Columbia, United States of America, with the chances of sudden death infinitely removed, shops plentifully stocked, motorcars still swarming, and the city of Washington spread out before him.

Crowe stirred a little uneasily. He hoped he had not been

brought to this land of plenty unnecessarily; he regretted already having left his flotilla and the eternal hunt after U-boats.

The car stopped and Harley sprang out and held the door open for him. There were guards in naval uniform round the door, revolvers sagging at their thighs; a desk at which they paused for a space.

'No exceptions,' smiled Harley, apologizing for the fact that not even the uniform of a British naval captain would let them into the holy of holies for which they were headed. There were two men in the room to which Harley led him.

'Good morning,' said the admiral.

'Good morning, sir,' said Crowe.

'Sorry to hurry you like this,' the admiral said gruffly. 'But it's urgent. Meet Lieutenant Brand.'

Brand was in plain clothes—seedy plainclothes. Crowe puzzled over them. Those clothes were the sort of suit that a middle-class Frenchman, not too well off, and the father of a family, would wear. And Brand's face was marked with weariness and anxiety.

'Brand left Lisbon about the same time you left London,' said the admiral. His eyes twinkled—no, 'twinkled' was too gentle a word—they glittered under thick black eyebrows. No man who looked into those eyes even for a moment would want to be the admiral's enemy. Now he shot a direct glance at Crowe, twisted his thin lips and shot a question.

'Supposing,' he asked, 'you had the chance to give orders to a U-boat captain, what orders would you give?'

Crowe kept his face expressionless. 'That would depend,' he said cautiously, 'on who the U-boat captain was.'

'In this case it is Korvettenkapitän Lothar Wolfgang von und zu Loewenstein.'

Captain Crowe repressed a start. 'I know him,' he said.

'That's why you're here.' The admiral grinned. 'Didn't they tell you in London? You're here because few people on our side of the ocean know Loewenstein better than you.'

Crowe considered. Yes, he decided, the admiral's statement was right. He knew Loewenstein. In the years before 1939, the German had made quite a reputation for himself by his bold handling of his yacht in English regattas—Loewenstein and his helmsman. Burke? Of course not. Bruch—Burch— something like that. Good man, that helmsman.

Crowe had met Loewenstein repeatedly on several formal occasions when the British navy had met detachments of the

German navy while visiting. And since 1939 their paths had crossed more than once—Crowe on the surface in his destroyer, and Loewenstein two hundred feet below in his submarine.

'Loewenstein,' the admiral was saying, 'left Bordeaux on the thirteenth—that's four days ago—with orders to operate on the Atlantic coast. We know he has four other U-boats with him. Five in all.'

The shaggy-browed admiral leaned over the desk. 'And Loewenstein,' he added, 'is out to get the *Queen Anne*.'

Captain Crowe blinked again.

'The *Queen Anne*,' pursued the American admiral ruthlessly, 'that is due to clear very shortly with men for the Middle East and India. Men we can't afford to lose. Not to mention the ship herself.'

'What's the source of your information, sir?' Captain Crowe asked.

'Brand here,' said the admiral, 'also left Bordeaux on the thirteenth.'

That piece of news stiffened Crowe in his chair and he stared more closely at the lieutenant in plain clothes. The news explained a lot—the seedy French suit, the hollow cheeks and the haggard expression. A man who had been acting as a spy in Bordeaux for the last six months would naturally look haggard.

Brand spoke for the first time and his pleasant Texan drawl carried even more than the hint that he had not only been speaking French but thinking in French for a long time.

'This is what I brought from Bordeaux,' he said, taking an untidy bundle of papers from the admiral's desk. 'It's the code the German agents in this country use for communications with the U-boats.'

Crowe took the bundle from his hand and gave it a cursory glance. This was not the time to give it prolonged study, complicated as it was, and half the columns were in German, which he did not understand. The other half were in English, and were composed of a curiously arbitrary sequence of words. Crowe caught sight of 'galvanized iron buckets' and 'canned lobster' and 'ripe avocados'. Farther down the column there were figures instead of words—apparently every value in American money from a cent to five dollars had a German equivalent, and the words 'pounds' and 'dozens' and even the hours of the day could convey certain meanings when put in their proper context.

'With that code,' explained Brand, 'you can give time, courses, latitude and longitude—anything you want.'

Crowe braved a question he half suspected he should not have asked. 'Where did you get this?'

'It's not the original,' interposed the admiral. 'The Nazis don't know we've got this. There's no missing original to give them the tip to change their code.'

'A French girl got it for me,' Brand explained.

There was a silence and then the admiral said, 'Well, Captain, there's the set-up. What have you to suggest?'

Captain Crowe looked down at the floor and then up at the admiral.

'Of course the *Queen Anne* will be secured by convoy,' he said. 'I know you're not thinking of letting her make her regular transport runs without escort. If Loewenstein is waiting for her with five submarines, her speed won't do her any good. And if the Germans know the course and time out of your ports now, there's no guaranteeing they won't know any change in course or time you might give the *Queen Anne*.'

The admiral made a sudden gesture. 'We can send the *Queen* out with half the fleet,' he said. 'But once we're at—map, please, Lieutenant!'

Young Harley spread a map in front of the admiral. Captain Crowe hunched over it, following the line pointed by the top-striper's finger.

'Once there,' said the admiral, 'we'll have to let the *Queen* go on her own. We can't go past that point without neglecting our coastal duties. And Loewenstein is bound to trail along until the escort leaves. Then he'll hit. Unless he can be drawn off.'

'Yes,' echoed Crowe absently. 'Unless we can draw him off.'

'Can we?' the admiral demanded. 'Or—I'm sorry—that's an unfair question, thrown at you all at once, Captain. Think it over and tomorrow morning at'—he glanced at his wristwatch—'ten we'll talk it over.'

'It wouldn't break my heart,' said the naval-intelligence agent, Brand, suddenly, 'if something drastic happened to Loewenstein. I've seen some of the pictures he's taken with his little camera from conning towers. Close-ups of drowning men—and one that's the pride of his collection, a woman and a kid off the *Athenia*.'

'Something drastic is going to happen to Loewenstein,' said the admiral. He looked at Crowe, and the captain blinked.

'Right-o,' said Captain Crowe.

He found himself outside the office without clearly realizing how he got there. He wanted to walk; he was urgently anxious to walk, partly because long hours in planes had cramped his legs—legs accustomed to miles of deck marching—and partly because he wanted to think—had to think—and he thought best on his feet.

He had to draw Loewenstein off. But what could draw a sub commander off a prize like the *Queen Anne*? To sink the *Queen* would give any U-boat skipper the *Pour le Mérite* with oak leaves or whatever brand of decoration Hitler was giving out now. A man would have to be mad to forsake a prize like that. Mad or—but Loewenstein had been half mad that day he had seized the wheel from his helmsman at that Copenhagen regatta and had tried to ram the boat that had overhauled him and blanketed him, stealing the race at the last moment. That Danish club had disbarred Loewenstein for that. But the helmsman had been exonerated. Good man, that helmsman, Crowe thought. Braucht—it was something that started with a *B*. Broening. Yes, that was it—Broening.

Crowe looked around him, squinted at the sun, tucked his chin in his limp white collar and set off boldly in the direction of the British Embassy. He was remembering all he could about Korvettenkapitän von und zu Loewenstein. He called up the slightly pug nose, the cold blue eyes, the colourless hair slicked back from the forehead—he remembered all these. Then there was the ruthless boldness with which he would jockey for position at the start of a yacht race. He would bear down on another boat, keeping his course while the helmsman—Broening—yelled a warning until the other boat fell off. The protest flags fluttered on many occasions when Loewenstein sailed. And after the races, it always was Loewenstein and some beautiful harpy at their table, alone, except for the miserable helmsman, Broening. Now, Loewenstein was the boldest of all U-boat captains.

Crowe knew his lips were not moving, but his mind was speaking. *Draw Loewenstein off*, it said. *But how? Loewenstein is a believer in the guns, as shown by his record. He conserves his torpedoes to the last. The ideal method of attack, according to Loewenstein, is to rise to the surface at night, preferably when there is just enough moon, or shore-light glare, to give a good silhouette of the target. He times his rise so that the convoy is almost upon him. Then he uses his guns furiously, pumping shells into every hull he can see; his whole pack of U-boats firing together. Then, before the escort comes up, even before the deck guns of the freighters can go into action, his sub flotilla submerges and scatters on divergent courses that confuse surface listening posts so that the escort destroyers don't know the exact spot over which to make their run. Damned clever—except he thinks the Americans don't know how he works. And I—God help me—have been brought over here to show Loewenstein he guessed wrong. But what is it about Broening that's so important? Why do I keep thinking about him?*

It would be eight or nine days before Loewenstein and his pack could be expected off the American coast. In that time the moon would be past its full. Three-quarters, rising about eleven. So that it might be best to—

Crowe forgot the sweat that dripped down his face—everything except the problem at hand. It was something that even in his wide experience he had not encountered before, this opportunity of sending orders to an enemy in the sure and certain knowledge that they would be received and acted upon.

Broening, he told himself. *Last I heard of him was that he'd become a Johnny come lately in the Nazi Party and Von Ribbentrop had sent him to some little Latin American country as a consul. Loewenstein must have loved that. Always hated the man, Loewenstein did, even though he won races for him. Now, despite all Loewenstein's Junker background, it seems that Broening is outstripping him in the race for prestige. I'll wager Loewenstein would like nothing better than to—I believe I have it.*

The shower bath offered him by a friend in need at the Embassy was something for which he would have given a month's pay. He stepped under the cold rain and pranced about solemnly while the healing water washed away the heat and his irritation. A plan to deal with Loewenstein was forming in his mind, and as he cooled down, his spirits rose and he nearly began to sing, until he remembered that he was on the dignified premises of the British Embassy. But he still grew happier and happier until he was struck by a fresh realization. Then his spirits fell abruptly. He had not written either to Susan or Dorothy this week, thanks to the hours spent travelling from England. And today was nearly over, and tomorrow he would have to write to Miriam—three letters pressing on him, to say nothing of the official report he would have to write. Crowe groaned and stayed under the shower a minute longer than he need have done in order to postpone the evil moment when he would have to come out and face a world in which letters had to be written, and when he did he was cursing himself for a soft-hearted fool for not cutting off the correspondence and saving himself a great deal of trouble.

But outside, the assistant naval attaché welcomed him with a smile.

'Here's Miss Haycraft,' he said. 'I thought you'd like her assistance in writing your report. You needn't worry about her—she knows more secrets than the Admiralty itself.'

Miss Haycraft was a pleasant little fair-haired thing with an unobtrusive air of complete efficiency. She sat down with her notebook in just the right way to start Crowe off pouring out his report of his interview with the admiral and Lieutenant Brand.

Half-way through his discourse, Captain Crowe stopped. 'I wonder if the Embassy has any records on a man named Broening?' he asked. 'Nazi fellow. Believe he was consul or minister or something in a Central American state. I—'

'Yes, Captain,' said Miss Haycraft crisply. 'Herr Broening is in New York, waiting to take passage on the diplomatic-exchange ship, *Frottingholm*.'

'Ah?' asked Crowe. 'And when does the *Frottingholm* sail?'

'It's not definite,' the girl answered. 'There's some trouble getting Berlin to assure safe passage.'

'Umm,' said Captain Crowe.

In another ten minutes the report was done. Crowe looked at Miss Haycraft and felt temptation—not temptation with regard to Miss Haycraft, however; she was not the girl to offer it.

'Was the A.N.A. really speaking the truth when he said you could be trusted with a secret?' he asked.

'Yes,' said Miss Haycraft, and her manner implied that there was no need at all to enlarge on the subject.

'All right then,' said Crowe, taking the plunge. 'Take this letter—Dear Susan: As you will see, I have got hold of a typewriter and I am trying my hand at it. Please forgive me this week for being so impersonal, but I have had a good deal to do. I wish you could guess where I am now; all I can say is I wish you were here with me because—'

The letter to Susan ran off as smoothly as oil; it was even more impressive than the writing of the report. When it was finished, Crowe looked at Miss Haycraft once more. Well, he might as well be hanged for sheep as for lamb.

'I'd like you,' he said, 'to do that letter over three times—no, you might as well make it four. Begin 'em "Dear Susan", "Dear Dorothy", "Dear Miriam" and "Dear Jane"—no, not "Dear Jane". You'd better say "Dearest Jane". Have you got that right?'

'Yes, Captain Crowe,' said Miss Haycraft, and she did not even smile.

This was marvellous; his conscience was clear for a week, and Crowe felt more like singing than ever, but he had to restrain himself. He did not mind letting Miss Haycraft into the secret of his epistolary amours, but singing in front of her was another matter. Perhaps it was the mounting internal pressure arising from the suppression of his desire that led to the rapid evolution in his mind of the plan to discomfit Loewenstein.

All I need, he told himself, *is an old hulk with a loose propeller shaft, a quick job of maritime face-lifting, and some co-operation from the newspaper and wireless Johnnies. I've a feeling the admiral ought to be able to get those things for me.*

'What can I do for you, Mr O'Connor?' asked the manager of the broadcasting station, after he had offered his unknown visitor a chair.

Mr O'Connor displayed a badge held in the palm of his hand and passed an unsealed envelope across the desk to the manager.

'Very glad to do anything I can,' said the head of the broad-casting station, when he read the enclosed letter.

Mr O'Connor produced a couple of typewritten sheets of paper.

'That goes on the air,' he said, 'at eleven o'clock tomorrow morning, at Reitz's usual time.'

The manager looked at the sheets. It was the usual kind of broadcast for which Mr Reitz paid twice a week, advertising the goods for sale in his store—galvanized buckets at sixty-nine cents. Grade A canned peaches at thirty-nine cents, and so on. The turns of phrase, the arrangement of the wording bore the closest poss-ible resemblance to Mr Reitz's usual style.

'I suppose I'll have to do it,' said the station manager. 'Glad to do anything to help, as I said. But what is Reitz going to say when he hears it?'

'He may hear it,' said O'Connor dryly, 'but he won't be in a position to object. He'll be in a safe place, and I don't expect it'll be long before he's in a safer place still.'

'I see,' said the station manager.

There was nothing more to be said on the subject of Mr Reitz's objections; it had all been said in those few words and in the glance of Mr O'Connor's hard eyes.

'All the same,' supplemented the FBI agent, 'I would prefer it if you did not discuss Reitz with anyone else.'

'Of course not,' said the man across the desk. 'And this will go on the air at eleven tomorrow morning.'

'Thank you very much,' said O'Connor, reaching for his hat.

'It will be a clear night, Captain,' said the admiral, coming up to the tiny bridge. 'That's the latest forecast.'

'I wouldn't object to a bit of haze myself, sir,' said Crowe.

'If you were in heaven,' chuckled the admiral, 'I'll bet you'd say your crown didn't fit and your harp was out of tune. But you must admit everything's come off slicker than an eel in a barrel of grease. There's the old *Peter Wilkes*, God bless her leaking hull, all dressed up in a coat of white paint and a big sign, DIPLOMAT, on her side, lighted up like a Coney Island excursion boat, wallowing along ahead of us with that fake second funnel threatening to blow off any minute. And her loose screw is kicking up such a fuss that our listeners are going deaf. And here we are, seven of us, coasting along behind that makeshift *Frottingholm*, blacked out and with our men at battle stations. I only hope your hunch is right, Captain. I'd hate to lose that skeleton crew aboard the *Wilkes*. And I'd hate to have this whole expedition turn out to be a howler.'

'It won't,' said Crowe, with an assurance he did not feel. 'Loewenstein hates Broening—always has. He knows if his former helmsman gets back to Berlin safely, Raeder is due to give him a naval command that would put him over Loewenstein. And Germany wants to break up Pan-American solidarity if she can. What better way than to have a U-boat sink a diplomatic ship and claim it was done by you Americans or we British? Loewenstein thinks he can kill two birds with one stone—getting rid of a personal enemy and staging a *cause célèbre* at the same time. And he won't torpedo that ship. He's been told it's without escort, so he'll surface and shell—and machine-gun the lifeboats later, at his convenience.'

'And the loose screw of the *Wilkes*,' observed the admiral, 'will prevent his listeners from knowing we're in the neighbourhood.'

'Right, sir.'

Crowe turned and looked back over the rigid line following behind him. He felt very happy at the imminent prospect of action. He was about to sing, when he remembered the presence of the admiral beside him. Admirals cramped one's style in a manner especially noticeable to a captain whose rank usually made him monarch of all he surveyed.

'Lord Jeffrey Amherst was a soldier of the King,' sang the admiral, as if he were doing it just to rub in the difference in rank. Then he broke off.

'You've no business here at all, you know.'

'None, sir,' agreed Crowe. 'But I'm not the only one like that on board.'

'Perhaps not,' grinned the admiral.

The sun was down now and the darkness was increasing rapidly. The false-faced *Frottingholm* lurched and staggered in the rising seas, a boldly lighted figure on a darkening seascape. The destroyer which Crowe rode rose and fell to the long Atlantic rollers. The men were at the guns. Down below, there were men with earphones clamped over their heads, trying to pick out the sound of submarine engines beneath the howl of the *Wilkes'* clattering screw. The ship, the whole little squadron, was keyed up, ready to explode into action. Somewhere in the darkness ahead was Loewenstein, rereading, perhaps, the information that had come to him that morning regarding the sailing of the *Frottingholm* with one August Broening aboard, the course and speed and destination of the diplomatic-exchange ship. No one could be quite sure of how Loewenstein would act on that information, but everything that Crowe knew about him led the captain to believe he would attack on the surface, about midnight, with his prey silhouetted against a nearly level moon. And, Crowe hoped, Loewenstein would use his deck guns to carry away the radio antenna first, so that no radio operator could tell the world that a ship carrying Nazi diplomats was being sunk by a German sub.

As always in the navy on active service, action would be preceded by a long and tedious wait. Crowe had learned to wait—years and years of waiting had taught him how.

A bell rang at length, sharply, in the chartroom behind him.

The admiral was inside on the instant, and Crowe overheard a low-voiced dialogue between him and the ensign within. Then the white uniform of the admiral showed up again, ghostly in the dark.

'They're onto something,' said the admiral. 'Can't get a bearing because of the ungodly noise that dressed-up hulk ahead is making. But I think your friend is in the neighbourhood.'

'I hope he is,' said Crowe. He was not merely hardened to waiting; he was hardened to disappointment by now.

'Yes,' said the admiral. Crowe was making himself stand still, and was snobbishly proud of the fact that the admiral did not seem able to do the same. Faint through the darkness Crowe could hear him humming, under his breath, 'Lord Jeffrey Amherst was a soldier of the King'.

Funny thing for an American admiral to be singing, Crowe told himself. Lord Jeffrey Amherst, he had never heard of him.

The bell rang again and yet again, and the information brought each time was more defined. Something on the port bow was moving steadily to intercept the *Wilkes*. And behind them rose the moon.

There was no chance at all of the squadron being surprised, but no one could tell just at which second the shock would come.

Somebody shouted. The gongs sounded. Crowe caught a fleeting glimpse of a long black shape breaching just off the side of the gaily lighted white bulk ahead. Then the guns broke into a roar, each report following the preceding one so closely as to make an almost continuous din. The flashes lit every part of the ship, dazzling the officers on the bridge. The destroyer was turning under full helm; not half a mile away there came a couple of answering flashes, lighting the sullen sea between. Then, as quickly as they had begun, the din and the flashes ceased. The little ship was leaping through the water now, the propeller turning at maximum speed, now that there was no need to deceive listeners at the instruments in the submarines. The squadron was spreading out fanwise in accordance with the drill so painfully learned during preceding years. Someone shouted another order, and the depth charges began to rain into the sea.

Then the destroyers wove together again and the last depth charges searched out the areas that had escaped the teeth of the comb in the first sweep. Reports were coming up from below in a steady stream. The little ship's consorts were sending messages as well.

'We hit two,' said the admiral. 'I saw the bursts.'

Crowe had seen them, too, but submarines have been known to survive direct hits from big shells. But if Loewenstein had been where he might have been expected to be, out watching the effect of his guns and the behaviour of his subordinates, there was every chance that one of the shells had killed him.

'Only negative from down below,' said the admiral.

The instruments probed the ocean depths unhampered, now that the *Wilkes* had cut her engines and was drifting. Reports said there was no trace of the solid bodies the instruments previously had contacted below the surface. Presumably, every submarine, torn open and rent asunder, had already sunk down into the freezing depths.

Crowe took the first full breath he had enjoyed since the admiral had flung his poser at him in the Navy Department office, days before. Now, he knew, the *Queen Anne* could make her run with relative security. Now he knew his hunch had been right: his hunch that Loewenstein would try to murder his helmsman, Broening.

The bell rang and some fresh information came up.

'Some indication of something on the surface. These things are too sensitive, if that's possible,' said the admiral. 'They tell you if a man spits over the side. This'll be wreckage, I guess . . . Listen!' he said suddenly. There was a voice hailing them from the surface. 'A survivor. One of the gun's crew blown into the sea when our shells hit them.'

Survivors sometimes can give even better information than wreckage. They searched carefully in the faint light of the moon to find the man who was hailing them. And when they found him and hauled him on board, Crowe recognized the pug nose and the shape of the head even through the mask of oil. It was Korvettenkapitän Lothar Wolfgang von und zu Loewenstein.

The Young Man from Kalgoorlie

I

He lived with his parents on a sheep-farm two hundred miles north-east of Kalgoorlie. The house was in the old style; a simple white wooden cabin to which a few extensions had been added by successive generations. On the low hills east of the farm there were a few eucalyptus trees; his mother grew pink and mauve asters under the house windows in summer; and in spring the wattle was in blossom everywhere, like lemon foam. All of his life had been lived there, and the war itself was a year old before he knew it had even begun.

On the bomber station, surrounded by flat grey English hills cropped mostly by sugar-beet and potatoes and steeped in winter-time in thick windless fogs that kept the aircraft grounded for days at a time, he used to tell me how it had come to happen that he did not know the war had started. It seemed that he used to go down to Kalgoorlie only once, perhaps twice, a year. I do not know what sort of place Kalgoorlie is, but it seemed that he did there, on that visit or so, all the things that anyone can do on a visit to almost any town in the world. He used to take a room for a week at a hotel, get up at what he thought was a late hour every morning—about eight o'clock—and spend most of the day looking at shops, eating, and then looking at shops again. In the evenings he used to take in a cinema, eat another meal, have a couple of glasses of beer in the hotel lounge and then go to bed. He confessed that it wasn't very exciting and often he was relieved to get back into the Ford and drive steadily back to the sheep-farm and the familiar horizon of eucalyptus trees, which after the streets of Kalgoorlie did not seem a bad prospect at all. The truth was that he did not know anyone in Kalgoorlie except an aunt, his mother's sister, who was very deaf and used a patent electrical acoustic device which always seemed to go wrong whenever he was there and which he had once spent more than a day trying to repair. He was very quiet and he did not easily get mixed up with people; he was never drunk and more than half the time he was worried that his father was making a mess of things at home.

It was this which was really the cause of his not knowing about the war. His father was an unimaginative and rather careless man to whom sheep were simply sheep and grass simply grass and who had kept sheep on the same two thousand acres, within sight of the same eucalyptus trees, for thirty years, and expected to go on keeping them there for the rest of his life. He did not understand that two years of bad luck had anything to do with his having kept sheep in the same way, on the same grass, for so long. It was the son who discovered that. He began to see that the native grasses were played out, and in their place he decided to make sowings of Italian rye-grass and subterranean clover; and soon he was able to change the flocks from one kind of grass to another and then on to a third and soon he could see an improvement in the health of every breed they had.

After that he was virtually in charge of the farm. His parents, who had always thought him a wonderful person, now thought him more wonderful still. When neighbours came—and this too was not often, since the nearest farm was another thirty miles up country—they talked of nothing but Albert's achievement. The sheep had improved in health, the yield of wool had increased, and even the mutton, they argued, tasted sweeter now, more like the meat of thirty years ago. 'Got a proper old-fashioned flavour,' his mother said.

It was about a year after these experiments of his—none of them very original, since he had simply read up the whole subject in an agricultural paper—that war broke out. It seemed, as he afterwards found out, that his mother first heard of it on an early morning news bulletin on the radio. She was scared and she called his father. The son himself was out on the farm, riding round on horseback taking a look at the sheep before breakfast. When he came in to breakfast he switched on the radio, but nothing happened. He opened up the radio and took a look at it. All the valves were warm, but the detector valve and another were not operating. It seemed a little odd but he did not take much notice of it. All he could do was to write to Kalgoorlie for the spare valves, and he did so in a letter which he wrote after dinner that day. It was three miles to the post-box and if there were any letters to be posted his mother took them down in the afternoon. His mother took this letter that afternoon and tore it up in little pieces.

That must have happened, he discovered, to every letter he wrote to the Kalgoorlie radio shop in the next twelve months. No valves ever came and gradually, since it was summer and sheep-shearing time and the busiest season of the year, the family got used to being without the radio. His father and mother said they even preferred it. All the time he had no idea of the things they were doing in order to keep the war from him. The incoming post arrived once a week and if there were any letters for him his mother steamed them open, read them and then put the danger-ous ones away in a drawer upstairs. The newspapers stopped coming, and when he remarked on it his father said he was tired of wasting good money on papers that were anyway nearly a week old before they came. If there were visitors his mother managed to meet them before they reached the house. In October the sheep-shearing contractors came and his father, ordinarily a rather careful man, gave every man an extra pound to keep his mouth shut. All through that summer and the following winter his mother looked very ill, but it was not until later that he knew the reason of it—the strain of intercepting the letters, of con-stantly guarded conversation, of warning neighbours and callers, of making excuses and even of lying to him, day after day, for almost a year.

The time came when he decided to go to Kalgoorlie. He always went there about the same time of the year, in late August, before the busy season started. His parents must have anticipated and dreaded that moment, and his father did an amazing thing. In the third week of August, early one morning, he put two tablespoon-fuls of salt in a cup of hot tea and drank it, making himself very sick. By the time Albert came in to breakfast his father was back in bed, very yellow in the face, and his mother was crying because he had been taken suddenly ill. It was the strangest piece of deception of all and it might have succeeded if his father had not overdone things. He decided to remain in bed for a second week, making himself sick every third or fourth day, knowing that once Septem-ber had come Albert would never leave. But Albert was worried. He did not like the recurrent sickness which now affected his father and he began to fear some sort of internal trouble.

'I'm going to Kalgoorlie whether you like it or not,' he said, 'to get a doctor.'

II

It was on the bomber station, when he had become a pilot, that he used to tell me of that first day in Kalgoorlie, one of the most remarkable in his life. When he left the farm his mother seemed very upset, and began crying. He felt that she was worried about his father; he was increasingly worried too and promised to be back within three days. Then he drove down to Kalgoorlie alone: perhaps the only man in Australia who did not know that the war was a year old.

He arrived at Kalgoorlie about four o'clock in the afternoon and the town seemed much the same as ever. He drove straight to the hotel he always stayed at, booked himself a room and went upstairs to wash and change. About five o'clock he came down again and went into the hotel lounge for a cup of tea. Except for a word or two with the cashier and the lift-boy he did not speak to a soul. He finished his tea and then decided to go to the downstairs saloon, as he always did, to get himself a haircut. There were several people waiting in the saloon, but he decided to wait too. He sat down and picked up a paper.

He must have gone on staring at that paper, not really reading it, for about ten minutes. It was late August and the Nazis were bombing London. He did not understand any of it; who was fighting or what were the causes of it. He simply took in, from the headlines, the story of the great sky battles, the bombing, the murder and destruction, as if they were part of a ghastly fantasy. For the moment he did not feel angry or sick or outraged because he had been deceived. He got up and went out into the street. What he felt, he told me, was very much as if you were suddenly to discover that you had been living in a house where, without knowing it, there was a carrier of smallpox. For months you have lived an ordinary tranquil life, unsuspecting and unafraid, and then suddenly you made the awful discovery that every fragment of your life, from the dust in your shoes to the air you breathed, was contaminated and that you had been living in danger. Because you knew nothing you were not afraid; but the moment you knew anything all the fears and terrors you had not felt in the past were precipitated into a single terrible moment of realization.

He also felt a fool. He walked up and down the street. As he passed shops, read placards, saw men in service uniform, fragmentary parts of his life during the past year became joined together, making sense: the broken radio, his unanswered letters, the newspapers, his mother's nervousness and the fact, above all, that they had not wanted him to come to Kalgoorlie. Slowly he understood all this. He tried to look on it as the simple cunning of country people. He was still too confused to be angry. But what he still did not understand, and what he had to find out about soon, was the war. He did not even know how long it had been going on. He stopped on a street-corner and bought another newspaper. The day before, he read, eighty-seven aircraft had been shot down over England. His hands were trembling as he read it, but it did not tell him the things he wanted to know. And he realized suddenly, as he stood there trembling in the hot sunshine, so amazed that he was still without feeling, that there was no means of knowing these things. He certainly could not know by asking. He imagined for a moment the effect of asking anyone, in the street, or the hotel, or back in the barber's saloon, a simple question like 'Can you tell me when the war began?'

He felt greatly oppressed by a sense of ridicule and bewilderment, by the fear that now, any time he opened his mouth, he was likely to make a ghastly fool of himself.

He walked about for an hour or more, pretending to look at shops, before it occurred to him what to do. Then it came to him quite suddenly that he would go and see the only other person he knew, who, like himself, could be cut off from the world of reality; the deaf aunt who lived in Kalgoorlie.

So he spent most of that evening in the old-fashioned parlour of her house, drinking tea, eating custard tarts, lightly brown with veins of nutmeg, and talking as steadily as he could into the electrical acoustic device fixed to the bodice of her dress. From such remarks as 'Things look pretty tough in England. Let's see, how long exactly has it been going on now?' he learned most of the elementary things he wanted to know. But there were still things he could not ask simply because he had no knowledge of them. He could not ask about France or Poland or Holland or Norway. All that he really understood clearly was that England and Germany were at war; that England was being bombed every day by great forces of aircraft; that soon, perhaps, she would be invaded. The simplicity and limitation of his knowledge was in a way, as he said, a good thing. For as he ate the last of the old lady's custard tarts and drank the last cup of tea and said good night to her he changed from being the man who knew least about the war in all Australia to the man who had perhaps the clearest, simplest, and most vivid conception of it in the whole continent. Forty years back his father and mother had emigrated from Lincolnshire to Kalgoorlie. Young, newly wed, and with about eighty pounds apart from their passage money, they started a new life. Now the roots of their existence, and so in a way the roots of his own existence, were being threatened with annihilation. This was the clear, simple, terrible thing he understood in such a clear, simple, terrible way.

When he got back to his hotel he drafted a telegram to his parents, telling them, as well as he could, that he understood. Then in the morning he went round to the nearest recruiting centre. I have not so far described what he was like. He was rather tall, fair, and brown in the face; his eyes were a cool blue and his lips thin, determined, and rather tight. He was just twenty-two and he had no way of holding back his anger.

'I want to be a pilot,' he said.

'All right,' they said. 'Good. But you can't be a pilot all of a sudden, just like that.'

'No?' he said. 'No? We'll bloody soon see.'

III

He adjusted himself as time went on but he carried some of his first angry, clear, terrible conceptions of things across the sea; across the Pacific to Vancouver, across the Atlantic to England. He was never angry with his parents and they in turn ceased being afraid about him. He used to describe to me how he went home on his first leave. From being stupidly affectionate in one way about him they became stupidly affectionate in quite another. They had not wanted him to go; now, because he had gone, they behaved as if they had everything to do with sending him and nothing to do with keeping him away. They had arranged a party and he said it was the largest gathering of folks anyone had ever seen on the farm. They invited everyone for thirty miles around and one or two people from fifty miles away. They killed several spring lambs and about fifteen fowls and tea was brewing all day long. At night they sang hymns and old songs in the drawing-room round the piano, and they slept in round beds on the floor. In the end he was almost glad to get away.

He promised to write to them often, and he promised also to keep a diary. He always did write and he always kept the diary. He sailed for Vancouver early in the year and by the spring he was flying Ansons and by the summer he was in England. It was an uncertain and rather treacherous summer and the harvest was wet and late in the corn country where we were. The potato fields were blighted, so that they looked as if spattered by drops of coffee on the dark rainy autumn days, and for long periods low cloud kept the aircraft down. Gradually the harvest fields were cleaned and the potatoes sacked and carted away, and in place of them you could see pale golden cones of sugar-beet piled in the fields and by the roadsides. I mention the weather because it was almost the only thing about England that troubled him. He longed for the hot dry air of the Australian summer and he used to tell me, as we gazed over the wet flat country, of the days when he had flown over Victoria in a Moth in his shirt sleeves and had looked down on the white beaches shining all along the coast in the sun.

The weather troubled him because his anger was still there. He felt that it frustrated him. He could never forget the day in Kalgoorlie when he had first read of the bombing and the mass murder in England and the very headlines of the paper had seemed like an awful dream. He felt that so much of his life had still to be brought up to date. Something had to be vindicated. Yet you could never tell that he was angry. It was easier to tell that he was sometimes afraid: not that he was afraid of dying or being hurt, but of some material thing like mishandling a kite. As he graduated from Moths to Ansons, to Blenheims and Wellingtons, and finally to Stirlings, he felt each time that he would never be big enough for the change to the bigger aircraft, yet it was always because of that fear that he was big enough.

Late that autumn he became captain of a Stirling and about the same time he got to know a girl. Two or three evenings a week, if there were no operations, we used to go down into the town and drink a few glasses of beer at a pub called the Grenadier, and one evening this girl came in. She was very dark and rather sophisticated, with very red lips, and she never wore her coat in the ordinary way but simply had it slung on her shoulders, with the sleeves empty and dangling. 'This is Olivia,' he said. For some reason I never knew her other name; we most often called her Albert's popsie, but after that, every night we were in the Grenadier, she would come in and soon, after talking for a time, they would go off somewhere alone together. The weather was very bad at that time and he saw her quite often. And then for a few nights it cleared and one night, before going to Bremen, he asked if I would keep his date with her and make his apologies and explain.

He had arranged to see her at seven o'clock and I made a bad impression by being late. She was irritable because I was late and because, above all, I was the wrong person.

'Don't be angry,' I said. 'I'm very sorry.'

'I'm not angry,' she said. 'Don't think it. I'm just worried.'

'You needn't be worried,' I said.

'Why not? Aren't you worried? You're his friend.'

'No, I'm not worried,' I said. 'I'm not worried because I know what sort of pilot he is.'

'Oh! you do, do you? Well, what sort of pilot is he?' she said. 'He never tells me. He never talks about it at all.'

'They never do,' I said.

'Sometimes I think I'll never know what sort of person he is at all. Never!'

I felt there was little I could say to her. She was angry because I was the wrong person and because she was frustrated. I bought her several drinks. For a time she was quieter and then once more she got excited.

'One night he'll get shot down and about all I'll know of him is that his name was Albert!'

'Take it easy,' I said. 'In the first place he won't get shot down.'

'No? How are you so sure?'

'Because he's the sort that shoots other people down first.'

'Are you trying to be funny?' she said.

'No,' I said; and for a few minutes I tried to tell her why it was not funny and why I had spoken that way. I tried quite hard but I do not think she understood. I realize that she knew nothing of all that had happened in Kalgoorlie; the blank year, the awful discovery about England, the bewilderment and the anger. I tried to make her see that there is a type that thinks of nothing but the idea that he may be shot at; and that there is another type, of which he was one, which thinks of nothing but shooting first. 'He's glad to go. He wants to go. It's what he lives for,' I said. 'Don't you see?'

No sooner had I said it than I realized that it was the stupidest thing in the world to say. It was herself, not flying, that she wanted him to live for. She did not understand, and it would have sounded very silly if I had tried to tell her, that he was engaged on something like a mission of vengeance, that because of all that had happened in Kalgoorlie, and especially that one day in Kalgoorlie, he felt that he had something damnable and cruel and hideous to wipe out from his conception of what was a decent life on earth. Every time he went up something was vindicated. Nor did she understand, and again it might have sounded foolish too, that it was the living and positive clarity of the whole idea that was really his preservation. All I could say was, 'He's the sort that goes on coming back and coming back until they're fed up with him and make him an instructor.'

Nevertheless, that night, her fears were almost justified. The flak over Bremen was very hostile and it seemed that he had to take a lot of hasty evasive action before he could get clear away along the coast. They had brought him down even then to about two thousand feet. The searchlights were very thick too and it was like daylight in the aircraft marking the time. But as if he couldn't possibly miss the opportunity, he came down to three hundred feet, roaring over the searchlight batteries as his gunners attacked them. They flew for about forty miles in this way, until finally something hit the outer starboard engine and holed the starboard wing. After that they were in a very bad way and got home, as he said, later than originally proposed.

I do not think he told her about this. It went down into his log and some of it may have gone down into the diary he had promised faithfully to keep for his people back on the farm. He was satisfied that he had blown out about twenty searchlights and that was all. Something else was vindicated. Two days later he had another go. In quite a short daylight attack along the Dutch coast he got into an argument with a flak ship. He was in a very positive mood and he decided to go down to attack. As he was coming in, his rear-gunner sighted a formation of Messerschmitts coming up astern, and two minutes later they attacked him. He must have engaged them for about fifteen minutes. He had always hated Messerschmitts and to be attacked by them made him very angry indeed. At the end of the engagement he had shot down two of them and had crippled a third, but they in turn had holed the aircraft in fifteen places. Nevertheless he went down just to carry out his instruction of giving the flak ship a good-bye kiss. She had ceased firing and he went in almost to low level and just missed her with his last two bombs by the stern. As he was coming home his outer port engine gave up, but he tootled in just before dark-ness, quite happy. 'A piece o' cake,' he said.

I know that he did not tell her about this either, and I could see that she had some excuse for thinking him undemonstrative and perhaps unheroic. For the next two days there was thick fog and rime frost in the early morning that covered the wings of the Stirlings with dusty silver. He was impatient because of the fog and we played many games of cribbage in the mess on the second day, while the crews were standing down.

On the third day he came back from briefing with a very satisfied look on his face. 'A little visit to Mr Salmon and Mr Gluckstein at Brest,' he said. He had been flying just a year. He had done twenty trips, all of them with the same meaning. It was a bright calm day, without cloud, quite warm in the winter sun. There were pools of water here and there on the runways and looking through the glasses I could see little brushy silver tails spurting up from the wheels of the aircraft as they taxied away.

When I looked into the air, again through the glasses, I saw two aircraft circling round, waiting to formate before setting course. One of them was smoking a little from the outer port engine. The smoking seemed to increase a little and then became black. Suddenly it seemed as if the whole engine burst silently and softly into crimson flower. I kept looking through the glasses, transfixed, but suddenly the aircraft went away behind the hangers as it came down.

That evening I waited until it was quite dark before going into the town. I went into the bar of the Grenadier and the girl was standing by the bar talking to the barmaid. She was drinking a port while waiting for him to come.

'Hullo,' she said. Her voice was cold and I knew that she was disappointed.

'Hullo. Could you come outside a moment?' I said.

She finished her port and came outside and we stood in the street, in the darkness. Some people went by, shining a torch on the dirty road, and in the light I could see the sleeves of her coat hanging loose, as if she had no arms. I waited until the people had gone by, and then, not knowing how to say it, I told her what had happened. 'It wasn't very heroic,' I said. 'It was damnable luck. Just damnable luck, that's all.'

I was afraid she would cry.

She stood still and quite silent. I felt that I had to do something to comfort her and I made as if to take hold of her arm, but I only caught the sleeve, which was dead and empty. I felt suddenly far away from her and as if we had known two different people: almost as if she had not known him at all.

'I'll take you to have a drink,' I said.

'No.'

'You'll feel better.'

'Why did it have to happen?' she said suddenly, raising her voice. 'Why did it have to happen?'

'It's the way it often does happen,' I said.

'Yes, it's the way it often does happen!' she said. 'Is that all you care? Is that all anyone cares? It's the way it happens!'

I did not speak. For a moment I was not thinking of her. I was thinking of a young man in a barber's saloon in Kalgoorlie, about to make the shocking discovery that the world was at war and that he did not know it.

'Yes, it's the way it happens!' she said. I could not see her face in the darkness, but her voice was very bitter now. 'In a week nobody will ever know he flew. He's just one of thousands who go up and never come back. I never knew him. Nobody ever knew him. In a week nobody will know him from anyone else. Nobody will even remember him.'

For a moment I did not answer. Now I was not thinking of him. I was thinking of the two people who had so bravely and stupidly kept the war from him and then had so bravely and proudly let him go. I was thinking of the farm with the sheep and the eucalyptus trees, the pink and mauve asters and the yellow spring wattle flaming in the sun. I was thinking of the thousands of farms like it, peopled by thousands of people like them: the simple, decent, kindly, immemorial people all over the earth.

'No,' I said to her. 'There will be many who will remember him.'

George MacDonald Fraser

Monsoon Selection Board

Our coal-bunker is old, and it stands beneath an ivy hedge, so that when I go to it in wet weather, I catch the combined smells of damp earth and decaying vegetation. And I can close my eyes and be thousands of miles away, up to my middle in a monsoon ditch in India, with my face pressed against the tall slats of a bamboo fence, and Martin-Duggan standing on my shoulders, swearing at me while the rain pelts down and soaks us. And all around there is mud, and mud, and more mud, until I quit dreaming and come back to the mundane business of getting a shovelful of coal for the sitting-room fire.

It is twenty years and more since I was in India. My battalion was down on the Sittang Bend, trying to stop the remnants of the Japanese Army escaping eastwards out of Burma—why we had to do this no one really understood, because the consensus of opinion was that the sooner Jap escaped the better, and good luck to him. Anyway, the war was nearly over, and one lance-corporal more or less on the battalion strength didn't make much difference, so they sent me out of the line to see if a War Office Selection Board would adjudge me fit to be commissioned.

I flew out and presented myself to the board, bush-hat on head, beard on chin, kukri on hip, all in sweaty jungle green and as tough as a buttered muffin. Frankly, I had few hopes of being passed. I had been to a board once before, back in England, and had fallen foul of a psychiatrist, a mean-looking little man who bit his nails and asked me if I had an adventurous spirit. (War Office Selection Boards were always asking questions like that.) Of course, I told him I was as adventurous as all get-out, and he helped himself to another piece of nail and said cunningly:

'Then why don't you sign on to sail on a Norwegian whaler?'

This, in the middle of the war, mark you, to a conscript. So, thinking he was being funny, I replied with equal cunning that I didn't speak Norwegian, ha-ha. He just loved that; anyway, I didn't pass.

So I flew out of Burma without illusions. This particular board had a tough reputation; last time, the rumour went, they had passed only three candidates out of thirty. I looked round at my fellow applicants, most of whom had at least three stripes and seemed to be full of confidence, initiative, leadership, and flannel— qualities that Selection Boards lap up like gravy—and decided that whoever was successful this time it wasn't going to be me. There were two other Fourteenth Army infantrymen, Martin-Duggan and Hayhurst, and the three of us, being rabble, naturally drifted together.

I should explain about Selection Boards. They lasted about three days, during which time the candidates were put through a series of written and practical tests, and the Board officers just watched and made notes. Then there were interviews and discussions, and all the time you were being assessed and graded, and at the finish you were told whether you were in or out. If in, you went to an Officer Cadet Training Unit where they trained you for six months and then gave you your commission; if out, back to your unit.

But the thing that was universally agreed was that there was no known way of ensuring success before a Selection Board. There were no standard right answers to their questions, because their methods were all supposed to be deeply psychological. The general view throughout the Army was that they weren't fit to select bus conductors, let alone officers, but that is by the way.

One of the most unpleasant features of a Selection Board was that you were on test literally all the time. At meal times, for instance, there was an examining officer at each table of about six candidates, so we all drank our soup with exaggerated care, offered each other the salt with ponderous politeness, and talked on a plane so lofty that by comparison a conversation in the Athanaeum Club would have sounded like an argument in a gin-mill. And all the time our examiner, a smooth, beady gentleman, kept an eye on us and weighed us up while pretending to be a boon companion.

It wasn't too easy for him, for at our second meal I displayed such zeal in offering him a bottle of sauce that I put it in his lap. I saw my chances fading from that moment, and by the time we fell in outside for our first practical test my nerves were in rags.

It was one of those idiotic problems where six of you are given a log, representing a big gun-barrel, and have to get it across a river with the aid of a few ropes and poles. No one is put in command; you just have to co-operate, and the examiners hover around to see who displays most initiative, leadership, ingenuity, and what-have-you. The result is that everyone starts in at once telling the rest what to do. I had been there before, so I let them argue and tried to impress the Board by being practical. I cleverly tied a rope round the log, and barked a sharp command to Martin-Duggan and Hayhurst. They tugged on the rope and the whole damned thing went into the river. At this there was a deadly silence broken only by the audible scribbling of the examiners, and then the three of us sheepishly climbed down the bank to begin salvage operations.

This set the tone of our whole performance in the tests. Given a bell tent to erect we reduced it to a wreck of cord and canvas inside three minutes; ordered to carry from Point A to Point B an ammunition box which was too heavy for one man and which yet did not provide purchase for two, we dropped it in a ditch and upbraided each other in sulphurous terms, every word of which the examiners recorded carefully. Asked to swing across a small ravine on a rope, we betrayed symptoms of physical fear, and Hayhurst fell and hurt his ankle. Taking all in all, we showed ourselves lacking in initiative, deficient in moral fibre, prone to recrimination, and generally un-officer-like.

So it went on. We were interviewed by the psychiatrist, who asked Hayhurst whether he smoked. Hayhurst said no—he had actually given it up a few days before—and then noticed that the psychiatrist's eyes were fixed on his right index finger, which was still stained yellow with nicotine. My own interview was, I like to think, slightly less of a triumph from the psychiatrist's point of view. He asked me if I had an adventurous spirit, and I quickly said yes, so much so that my only regret about being in the Army was that it prevented me from signing on to sail on a Norwegian whaler.

If, at this point, he had said: 'Oh, do you speak Norwegian, then?' he would have had me over a barrel. But instead he fell back on the Selection Board classic, which is: 'Why do you want to be an officer?'

The honest answer, of course, is to say, like Israel Hands, 'Because I want their pickles and wines and that,' and to add that you are sick of being shoved around like low-life, and want to lord it over your fellow-man for a change. But honest answer never won fair psychiatrist yet, so I assumed my thoughtful, stuffed look, and said earnestly that I simply wanted to serve the army in my most useful capacity, and I felt, honestly, sir, that I could do the job. The pay was a lot better, too, but I kept that thought to myself.

He pursed up and nodded, and then said: 'I see you want to be commissioned in the—Highlanders. They're a pretty tough bunch you know. Think you can handle a platoon of them?'

I gave him my straight-between-the-eyes look which, coupled with my twisted smile, tells people that I'm a lobo wolf from Kelvinside and it's my night to howl. Just for good measure I added a confident, grating laugh, and he asked with sudden concern if I was going to be sick. I quickly reassured him, but he kept eyeing me askance and presently he dismissed me. As I went out he was scribbling like crazy.

Then there were written tests, in one of which we had to record our instant reactions to various words flashed on a blackboard. With me there was not one reaction in each case, but three. The first was just a mental numbness, the second was the reaction which I imagined the examiners would regard as normal, and the third (which naturally was what I finished up writing down) was the reaction which I was sure would be regarded as abnormal to a degree. Some people are like this: they are compelled to touch naked electric wiring and throw themselves down from heights. Some perverse streak makes them seek out the wrong answers.

Thus, given the word 'board', I knew perfectly well that the safe answer would be 'plank' (unless you chose to think that 'board' meant 'Selection Board', in which case you would write down 'justice', 'mercy', or 'wisdom'). But with the death wish in full control I had to write down 'stiff'.

Similarly, reason told me to react to 'cloud', 'father', and 'sex' by writing down 'rain', 'W.G. Grace', and 'birds and bees'. So of course I put down 'cuckoo', 'Captain Hook', and 'Grable'. To make matters worse I then scored 'Grable' out in a panic and wrote 'Freud', and then changed my mind again, scoring out 'Freud' and substituting 'Lamour'. Heavy breathing at my elbow at this point attracted my attention, and there was one of the examiners, peeking at my paper with his eyes bugging. By this time I was falling behind in my reactions, and was in such a frenzied state that when they eventually flashed 'Freud' on the board I think my response was 'Father Grable'. That must have made them think.

They then showed us pictures, and we had to write a story about each one. The first picture showed a wretch, with an expression of petrified horror on his face, clinging to a rope. Well, that was fairly obviously a candidate escaping from a Selection Board and discovering that his flight was being observed by a team of examiners taking copious notes. Then there was a picture of a character with a face straight out of Edgar Allan Poe, being apprehended by a policeman. (Easy: the miscreant was the former principal of a Selection Board, cashiered for drunkenness and embezzlement, and forced to beg his bread in the gutter, being arrested for vagrancy by a copper who turned out to be a failed candidate.)

But the one that put years on all the many hundreds of candidates who must have regarded it with uninspired misery was of an angelic little boy sitting staring soulfully at a violin. There are men all over the world today who will remember that picture when Rembrandt's Night Watch is forgotten. As art it was probably execrable, and as a mental stimulant it was the original lead balloon. Just the sight of that smug, curly-headed little Bubbles filled you with a sense of gloom. One Indian candidate was so affected by it that he began to weep; Hayhurst, after much mental anguish, produced the idea that it was one of Fagin's apprentices gloating over his first haul; my own thought was that the picture represented the infant Stradivarius coming to the conclusion that given a well-organized sweat-shop there was probably money in it.

Only Martin-Duggan dealt with the thing at length; the picture stirred something in his poetic Irish soul. The little boy, he recorded for the benefit of the examiners, was undoubtedly the son of a famous concert violinist. His daddy had been called up to the forces during the war, and the little boy was left at home, gazing sadly at the violin which his father would have no opportunity of playing until the war was over. The little boy was terribly upset about this, the thought of his father's wonderful music being silenced; he felt sure his daddy would pine away through being deprived of his violin-playing. Let the little boy take heart, said Martin-Duggan; he needn't worry, because if his daddy played his cards right he would get himself promoted to the post of quartermaster, and then he would be able to fiddle as much as he liked.

Martin-Duggan was terribly pleased with this effort; the poor sap didn't seem to understand that in military circles a joke is only as funny as the rank of its author is exalted, and Martin-Duggan's rank couldn't have been lower.

Of course, by the time the written tests were over, the three of us were quite certain that we were done for. Our showing had probably been about as bad as it could be, we thought, and our approach to the final ordeal of the Selection Board, on the third afternoon, was casual, not to say resigned. This was a trip over the assault course—a military obstacle race in which you tear across country, climb walls, swing on ropes, crawl through tunnels, and jump off ramps. The climax is usually something pretty horrid, and in this case it consisted of a monsoon ditch four feet deep in water, at the end of which was a huge bamboo fence up which you had to climb in three-man teams, helping each other and showing initiative, intelligence, cheerfulness, and other officer-like qualities, if possible.

We were the last three over, and as we waded up the ditch, encouraging each other with military cries, the rain was lashing down something awful. There was a covered shelter overlooking the ditch, and it was crammed with examiners—all writing away as they observed the floundering candidates—as well as the top brass of the board. All the other candidates had successfully scaled the fence, and were standing dripping with mud and water, waiting to see how we came on.

Our performance, viewed from the bank, must have been something to see. I stood up to my waist in water against the fence, and Martin-Duggan climbed on my shoulders, and Hayhurst climbed on his, and I collapsed, and we all went under. We did this about five or six times, and the gallery hooted with mirth. Martin-Duggan who was a proud, sensitive soul, got mad, and swore at me and kicked me, and Hayhurst made a tremendous effort and got on to the top of the fence. He pulled Martin-Duggan up, and the pair of them tried to pull me up, too, but I wasn't having any. I was rooted up to my middle in the sludge, and there I was going to stay, although I made it look as though I was trying like hell to get up.

They tugged and strained and swore, and eventually Martin-Duggan slipped and came down with a monumental splash, and Hayhurst climbed down as well. The spectators by this time were in hysterics, and when we had made three or four more futile efforts—during which I never emerged from the water once—the officer commanding the board leaned forward and said:

'Don't you chaps think you'd better call it a day?'

I don't know what Martin-Duggan, a mud-soaked spectre, was going to reply, but I beat him to it. Some heaven-sent inspiration struck me, because I said, in the most soapy, sycophantic, Eric-or-Little-by-Little voice I have ever used in my life:

'Thank you, sir, we'd prefer to finish the course.'

It must have sounded impressive, for the C.O. stood back, almost humbly, and motioned us to continue. So we did, floundering on with tremendous zeal and getting nowhere, until we were almost too weary to stand and so mud-splattered that we were hardly recognizable as human beings. And the C.O., bless him, leaned forward again, and I'll swear there was a catch in his voice as he said:

'Right, that's enough. Well tried. And even if you didn't finish it, there's one thing I'd like to say. I admire guts.' And all the examiners, writing for dear life, made muted murmurs of assent.

What they and the C.O. didn't know was that my trousers had come off while we were still wading up the ditch, and that was why I had never budged out of the water and why we had never got up the fence. A good deal I had endured, but I was not going to appear soaked and in my shirt-tail before all the board and candidates, not for anything. And as we waded back down the ditch and out of sight round the bend, I told Martin-Duggan and Hayhurst so.

And we passed, I suppose because we showed grit, determination, endurance, and all the rest of it. Although with Selection Boards you never could tell. Only the three of us know that what got us through was the loss of my pants, and military history has been made out of stranger things than that.

Alan Green

Turning Point

Robert lay on his back on the short, dry turf watching the vapour trails high above him. Every day for the past few weeks, he had clambered up the hill from the village to his favourite vantage point at the edge of Coppins Wood where he sat and looked on as the RAF confronted the German air armadas. At first he had been frightened, not daring to venture beyond the tree line; he had skulked close to the protective trunks, peering through the branches into the brilliant azure arena of the summer sky. He quickly realized, however, that the panorama being painted above him was much too big and exciting to be squinted at from behind a shield of such doubtful efficiency so he found a viewing position in a small grassy hollow, a few yards away from the trees, which afforded him an unrestricted view of the battles taking place overhead. And there, stretched out comfortably on the grass, he had seen sights that few boys of twelve could ever have expected.

He had seen German bombers come in from the east so low that at first he had thought they were lorries moving down the valley. He had seen swarms of them very high, etching their arrogant paths in straight white lines across the vaulted sky. Time and again, he had seen those lines waver, twist and curl before finally turning back in the direction from which they had come; and somehow, when that happened, all the pride proclaimed by their direct assault over the green fields of England was lost. He had seen crashes and men die. But to a small boy, for whom nothing in the world could be more exciting, these deaths had not been horrible and tragic. His father had said, in a very serious talk before he went to France, that many people on both sides were likely to die before things were settled.

'But why is there a war, Daddy? It's wrong to kill people, isn't it?'

'Usually it is, Robert, but now there is great danger. The Germans are trying to take over our world. They want to control us, to make us do what they want and to stop us doing what we want.

This is a war for freedom, for decency, for standards of right and wrong. And decent people must be prepared to kill—and to be killed—in defending those standards.'

'But, Daddy, why must you go to the war?'

'I have to, son. I am old enough to be a soldier. You aren't. But you will be responsible for looking after Mummy and the house while I am away.'

'Miss Whittaker makes me do things I don't want to at school.'

'That's different,' laughed his father. 'She makes you do things because they are right. When you are older, you will understand. But when somebody tries to make you do something that you know, really know, is very wrong indeed then killing, as in a war, may be the only way to protect the things you love most.'

As he lay on the grass watching the patterns of combat developing over his head, he remembered those words from his father and he thought of Mr Capstick. He had never met, or even heard of, Mr Capstick until those dreadful days towards the end of May. He knew the war was going badly and listened with his mother to the news bulletins, which always spoke of heroic resistance and British withdrawals. There was no word from his father, and his mother became more and more worried, although she tried to remain cheerful and confident when with him. One awful morning, though, there was a ring at the doorbell and there stood old Mr Jameson from the post office. Mutely he held out the telegram and both he and Robert watched as, hesitantly and trembling, she opened it and read the few words of the message. Leaning against the door-post, with her eyes closed and with the hand still clutching the telegram pressed against her forehead, she whispered, 'He's posted as missing.'

Robert eventually understood what that meant. It was a bit like his cricket ball which had rolled into the edge of Colonel Larkin's garden. He knew where it was or, rather, where he had last seen it and it was probably all right. But he hadn't exactly been able to find it so he couldn't say for sure it was 'missing'. One day he would find it and everything would be back to normal. Until then, however, it was a worry and a nuisance.

His mother certainly found it a worry and a nuisance. She read the newspaper from cover to cover every day; she listened incessantly to the wireless and made innumerable telephone calls. None of this had any result, though, and she was rapidly losing all hope of ever seeing her husband again when, on the last day of May, her sister telephoned. Aunt Jessie lived in Ramsgate and they often used to visit her before the war, having fun on the beach and watching the boats in the harbour. Now, the harbour was being used for very serious business, as the boats were ferrying back the remnants of the British Army from Dunkirk. Aunt Jessie rang to say that some of the boats had brought back men of the Buffs and there was just a chance that some of them might know what had happened to his father. Could she come over right away?

She could and she did, in a fever of anticipation as the train chugged on its way through Canterbury to the Kent coast. The front was crammed with people watching the soldiers, dirty, exhausted and some wounded, coming ashore from the vessels which had lifted them from the French beaches. Reception areas had been set up on the quayside and long queues of weary soldiers straggled past the trestle tables, reporting their names and units, before handing in their weapons and making their way to the waiting buses and trains. His mother forced her way through the crush and ran to the nearest reception point, where a dapper captain was supervising the cataloguing of this sorry residue of a once proud army.

'Please,' she said anxiously, 'Where are the Buffs coming ashore?'

'Madam,' he replied, 'We have men from every regiment of the British Army coming through here and some from regiments I have never heard of. The whole thing is a mess and I'm afraid we haven't time to deal with queries from civilians. Please contact the War Office if you have a problem.'

With that, he turned away and strode off through the mêlée surrounding his makeshift office. Downcast, she walked away and found herself face to face with Mr Capstick. He was arranging things. In fact, Robert came to realize later on that Mr Capstick was always arranging things. One of the first things he had arranged was reserved occupation status for himself. He owned a small engineering factory outside Broadstairs, which had originally made light alloy parts for motor cars and tractors. Shortly before the outbreak of war, production was switched to aeroengine components and Mr Capstick became much more valuable to the war effort in his civilian capacity than he ever would in uniform. The fact that he also became rather rich and influential was much appreciated by Mr Capstick who acknowledged that in these very difficult times, he was doing rather nicely. This showed in the snappy clothes he wore, in the Bentley he drove with, seemingly, unlimited supplies of petrol and in the small manor house he owned just outside Canterbury. That day at Ramsgate, he was supervising a small kitchen he had set up on the quay to provide tea, soup and sandwiches for the troops. Nobody could deny that Mr Capstick was always to the fore in offering his services to the country but few would be able to say with their hands on their hearts that he always made his offers of help for purely unselfish reasons. Many, in fact, would have put it even stronger, maintaining that Roger Capstick would do nothing for anybody unless he was going to get something out of it. Quite what he expected to get from his efforts to help the return of the Expeditionary Force was not clear, least of all to himself. But he had a nose for an opportunity and the homecoming of a bedraggled army was unlikely to present no chance at all. What he certainly had not counted on was meeting a lonely, desperate and very attractive woman.

He was all solicitude. Quick to recognize the distress and anguish she was going through and realizing that she was even more beautiful than he had at first thought, he turned on his charm.

'Can I help at all?' he said. 'I have a little influence around here and I might be able to manage something that the army doesn't have time for today.'

'Oh, please,' she sobbed. 'My husband is missing in France. I want to find someone in the Buffs to see if they know what might have happened to him.'

Tears streamed down her face as she gave in to her anxiety and stood helplessly appealing in front of Roger Capstick. True to his reputation, he arranged matters. First he took her over to his hard-working tea ladies and gave her a pint mug, the rim of which was chipped and showed clear evidence of previous use. Then he sat her down beside the counter and set about finding out just who it was she was looking for. Robert listened in silence to his mother as she spoke about Captain Archer of B Company, 3rd Battalion of the Royal East Kents. That description didn't seem to have very much to do with his Dad, who worked in Canterbury during the week but who played the most marvellous games of cricket with him at the weekend and who took him to the seaside and helped him with his homework. Captain Archer was 'missing'; but his Dad was just away for a short time, leaving him, Robert, to protect his mother. Mr Capstick listened attentively and then, saying that he would be as quick as he could, he disappeared into the surrounding mass of soldiery. Robert and his mother sat isolated in the sea of people, hardly daring to hope that within the multitude there was somebody who would be able to say just what had happened to the man in their lives.

In a remarkably short time, Capstick reappeared with a dirty and tousled squaddy in tow. He had no tunic or cap and his face was so oil stained that it was difficult to tell at first glance that he was an Englishman and not a foreign soldier. How Capstick had identified him as a Buff was a mystery, which became near miraculous when it became clear that not only was he a Buff but he was actually a member of Captain Archer's company and had been with him on the day he went missing.

'Mrs Archer, this is Private Yates. I believe he can tell you something about your husband.' Capstick then indicated to the tired and scruffy soldier that he should say his piece.

'Lady, I'm sorry about your 'usband,' he began. 'Good officer 'e was. Straight and fair. You can't ask for more than that. A few of us, with the Captain in charge, was supposed to try and stop Jerry on the road about 30 miles from Dunkirk. We was just getting into position and the Captain and a couple of the others 'ad gone forward to see what was what. Then there was a Gawd almighty bang from just over the 'ill where they was and we didn't see no more of 'em. We 'ung about for a while but there weren't much sense in waiting for Jerry to get us too, so we scarpered. None of us saw the Captain again and I should say that ol' Jerry whizz-bang got 'im fair and square. Reckon 'e would 'ave come back to us if 'e could. Not like 'im to leave us in the lurch so 'e's a goner, I'm afraid. Sorry to 'ave to say so, lady, but you better not count on 'im turning up 'ere.'

'But you don't know that he is actually . . .' she paused. 'He may have only been wounded and taken prisoner when the Germans moved forward. That's possible, isn't it?' she asked with desperate urgency.

'Lady, all things is possible. But some are just less likely than others. I wish you luck, I really do. But I got to go now.' With a friendly smile of encouragement he turned about and pressed his way through the crowd of clamouring, thirsty troops. Mr Capstick moved quietly to the distressed woman.

'Mrs Archer, I think it will not be very good for you, or serve much purpose, to stay here at the harbour very much longer. You will only upset yourself and I don't think there is anything else to learn. Let me take you home. My car is just a few yards away and I can easily leave somebody to look after my bits and pieces here.'

'Yes. Perhaps you are right,' she replied in a controlled but strained voice. 'But please don't bother yourself. I live the other side of Canterbury and I can go back on the train, the way I came.'

'I think you will find that all of the trains are now being used to take the soldiers off to their camps; and most of the buses too, so I really think you will be better off if you let me drive you.'

Too tired and depressed to argue any further, Robert's mother allowed herself to be led off by Mr Capstick, he lightly supporting her by the arm, with Robert holding firmly on to her other hand. The Bentley was large, comfortable and fast; it seemed hardly any time at all before they were turning into the familiar high street of their own village. Not all the apparent swiftness of the journey was accounted for by the car, splendid though it was. Mr Capstick was the perfect companion. Kind, considerate, intelligent, witty yet caring, he filled the ride with a warmth and understanding that they both desperately needed. He saw them into the house, made sure she could cope overnight and then left, promising to see how she was the next morning.

He telephoned that morning—and came out to the house in the afternoon. The same thing happened the next day. And the next. And the one after that. In fact, after that eventful visit to Ramsgate, Mr Capstick assumed a central role in their lives. He was always in contact; he was often actually present. And with his help, his companionship and his cheerful support he rapidly became indispensable. Within a week he had said, 'Please may I call you Jean? We seem to know each other so well already. If you will call me Roger, perhaps young Robert here will come to think of me as another uncle.'

So Jean, Roger and Uncle Roger it had become—except for Robert who never spoke or thought of their newly arrived friend as anything other than Mr Capstick. He was not used to strangers grafting themselves onto what, until the tragedy of the war, had been a very close-knit family. He was bewildered and a little apprehensive, particularly when, as at times it proved inevitable, he was told what to do by this man who had appeared as if from nowhere. During the days immediately after the news that his father was missing, and before the visit to the dockside during the evacuation, Robert had been very close to his mother. She had taken to discussing with him the worries and problems she would normally have talked over with his father. He did not understand everything she said but he gravely accepted the fact that he was now the man of the house and that he had a duty to receive these confidences from his mother. With Mr Capstick's arrival, this changed. Robert was too young to understand that adults tend to exclude children from what they see as serious matters but he resented the fact that decisions were made without his participation and, sometimes, against what he thought to be his best interests. He was stopped from visiting Jenkins in the cow parlour for the evening milking because Mr Capstick thought it unfair on his mother that his shoes were often soiled with fresh cow dung when he returned. He was not allowed to leave scraps of food and saucers of milk at the back door for his family of hedgehogs in case it encouraged vermin to attack the garden. He was not allowed to go swimming in the river without an adult to see that he didn't get into difficulties. To him, these were serious matters; but even they paled into insignificance against the change in the personal relationship between his mother and Mr Capstick. The early use of the Christian name and the gentlemanly touch on the arm when he first escorted her to his car had progressed at astonishing speed. They smiled into each other's eyes; they called one another 'Dear'; they linked arms when walking, providing they were sure not to meet anyone they knew. And once, Robert had walked into the kitchen unexpectedly to find them standing as though Mr Capstick had hurriedly released her from his arms. They stared at him without speaking and he was almost certain that they had been kissing when he came in. That did not seem right or fair. Daddy was in France somewhere, perhaps not very well and perhaps captured by the Germans. Mummy had been upset and frightened when it happened and had needed a grown-up to talk to and to help her sort things out. That much he could accept. But Mr Capstick was not in the war; he had not gone to France, nor had he been blown up by a German whizz-bang. He was rich, comfortable and safe. And that gave him no right to try to take Daddy's place, kissing Mummy and ordering people around. Some things in life were going horribly wrong and through the glorious summer days of August and September, while Robert watched the aerial battles being fought in the skies above his home, he gave considerable thought to the personal struggle going on within his family.

It was very hot on Saturday and Robert could not get off to sleep that night. The excitement of the day's battles was still with him so, restless and thirsty, he got out of bed and crossed the landing to the bathroom to have a drink of water. As he passed the top of the stairs he realized that his mother and Mr Capstick were standing at the front door and, without consciously deciding to do so, he paused to listen to their conversation. They were bidding each other good night and their final words came clearly to him as he peered through the banisters into the hall.

'You will tell him tomorrow, darling,' said his mother. 'He may accept that boarding school is a good idea when you explain that it is for his own good in getting him away from Kent in case the Germans do invade. But selling this house and moving into yours will not be very popular with him, to say the least.'

'Don't worry. I can handle him. He will do what I tell him and everything will be all right,' Capstick replied.

The remainder of their quiet endearments and the parting kiss went unnoticed by the stunned boy. So this was what it had come to! He was to be sent away to school while Mr Capstick got rid of Daddy's house and made Mummy forget all about Daddy and go and live with him. He was too overwhelmed to cry; silently miserable, he crept away to the reassuring surroundings of his own room where he took stock of this dreadful threat to all the things he loved most. He did not yet have the worldly experience to make allowance for irrational passion in working out how human decisions were reached. He could only assume that some- how Mr Capstick had forced his mother to believe that his father was dead and that he, Robert, was too much of a nuisance to keep at home. He agonized over the situation for most of the night and, again and again, he remembered his father saying that decent people must be prepared to fight for what they considered right. As dawn was breaking, he decided that there was only one way for him to protect his family.

Slipping silently from his bed, he tip-toed downstairs to the study and across to his father's desk. He knew that the locked top left-hand drawer contained a revolver. He had heard his father explain to his mother that it was there if ever she should need to defend herself against intruders. He also knew that the key of the bureau, just across the room from the desk, opened the drawer. Indeed, sometimes when he had been alone in the house he had taken out the gun, handling it and gazing at it in macabre fascina- tion. This time, along with the weapon, he removed the box of ammunition that was kept with it and crept quickly back upstairs. He had never loaded a gun before so it took him some time to put six rounds into the cylinder but he finally managed it before stuffing the weapon into his gas-mask case. The discarded mask he hid in the bottom of his toy cupboard.

At breakfast on Sunday morning he was quiet and tired, ans- wering in monosyllables his mother's attempts at conversation. She too, was tense and it was with some relief that she heard him say he was going to the Downs to see what was going on. Kissing him on the cheek, she told him to be careful and not to go away from his usual place.

'Uncle Roger will probably come and find you there later on,' she called after him as he set off along the lane, with the heavy gas-mask case banging against his hip.

Mr Capstick came to him just before one o'clock, by which time Robert had watched at least three enemy raids broken up by British fighters, who seemed to his by now expert eye to have sent rather more German aircraft than usual fleeing to the east, trailing smoke. It had been so exciting that Robert had almost forgotten the true purpose of his expedition when he heard Mr Capstick's voice say from behind him, 'Seems like a busy Sunday for mid-September. How are we doing?'

'Pretty good,' said Robert, his enthusiasm draining away. There was a long pause.

'Well, make the most of it, young man, because your mother and I have decided that, for your own good, you should . . .'

He stopped short, in mid-sentence, as the quiet of the hillside was shredded by the scream of a doomed aeroplane hurtling into the woods just behind them. Robert was aware only of a tremendous noise and a blast of hot air that hurled him headlong into the grassy hollow, where he lay dazed and terrified. When he recovered sufficiently to clamber to his feet, he could see that a fire had started amongst the trees. There was an overpowering smell of rubber and petrol and a dense pall of smoke was rising into a column of grey and black against the clear blue sky. Hundreds of pieces of wreckage were scattered over the field and amongst them, not far away, lay Mr Capstick. He was spreadeagled, face down, on the ground with his usually immaculate clothes scorched, rumpled and dirty. Sticking out of his back was a splintered branch from a tree impaling him securely to the short green turf. Robert walked unsteadily over to him, registering without emotion that he was, beyond any doubt, dead. Of the gas-mask case and its clandestine load there was no trace. The sudden sound of a low flying aircraft, very close, jolted Robert from his reverie and he dropped to his knees in fright. A Spitfire zoomed into view over the woods and circled the scene of its recent triumph. Robert could see the pilot quite clearly through the perspex of the cockpit canopy and he saw the gloved hand rise in salute to him before the sleek fighter climbed away to resume freedom's battle.

At the foot of the hill, he could see people starting to run towards the crash; among them he recognized his mother. Slowly he started walking down to meet her, knowing that this day was a turning point for them all.

Uys Krige

Death of the Zulu

It was about two hours after our capture. We were marching from Figtree towards Tobruk port. It was midsummer, the sun well up, but, thank God, not too hot yet—though I knew by the brittle cobalt look of the sky that it would not be long before the heat would become unbearable, beating down upon that bone-dry earth in shimmering, scorching waves ... We weren't doing anything, not even thinking, just trudging alone, dragging our heavy feet through the sand, raising the dust in yellowish-grey clouds in the dips and in little lingering puffs round our boots on the straight.

I appeared to have two minds: the one stunned, the other perfectly conscious, taking in coolly and dispassionately our surroundings. Only one sight was clear-cut, vivid: that silent mob of men streaming towards Tobruk. And only one sound audible: the click or scrunch of desert boots when we struck a rock vein or a loose surface of grit across our path.

Those boots, that everlasting dragging, clogged tramp, tramp, tramp ... Like a drum ... Like the slow, dull, monotonous beat of a drum. And with a single monotonous refrain: out of nothing, through nothing, towards nothing ... Out of nothing: the thunderous vacuum of the battle. Through nothing: this strange, unreal scene, as if flickering in a film. Towards nothing: the huge inconceivable emptiness of our life of captivity and exile to come ...

It would be more accurate to say I seemed to have, not two minds, but three, the third listening to a monologue by the conscious mind. 'Yes, before it often seemed to you,' it was saying, 'that you were living only in the past or the future, never in the present. The present was always escaping you, slipping like sand through your fingers. Now you have your present, my body, and a fine present it is too! Very present, very real ... And you can't barricade yourself against it by drawing on your memories. They've been washed out. Nor can you throw up a rampart against it with hopes, plans for the future. For your future, too, has gone down the drain. There is no past. There is no future. There's only the present . . .'

There were bodies lying beside the road, some singly, some in batches. Dead or wounded, I didn't look, I wasn't interested. My eyes slid over them as if they were so many pieces of old motor junk scattered about a disused yard somewhere. 'They're dead and they've a wife like you . . .' I heard a faint voice whisper somewhere far off. 'They're dead and they've a mother like you . . .' The voice was taking shape, getting stronger. 'They're dead and they've a child like you . . .' The voice, now, was quite loud. It was my unconscious mind awaking; and the monologue had become a dialogue.

'I don't care a damn . . .' I heard the calm mind say, but it was fast losing its imperturbability. 'Let them all go to hell . . . Let them all go straight to hell! I don't care a damn!'

Below the escarpment the track we were following made a curve. I was on the left-hand side of the curve when I heard a shout. Mechanically I looked up. To the right, in the curve's bulge, about fifty yards away, a German officer was standing over someone stretched out on the ground. He shouted again, beckoned with his arm. Though there must have been at least a dozen men in our group, numbly, apathetically, I thought: 'It's me he wants, he's looking straight at me, I can see the blue of his eyes . . .'

Automatically I stepped off the track. There were two other South Africans beside me also walking towards the German. I did not know who they were, I had never seen them before. They must have been beside me—or just behind me—during that long, weary trek from Figtree, but I hadn't noticed them. It was only now as, one on each side of me, they too moved forward towards the officer and the figure at his feet, that their presence began imping-ing upon my consciousness. And though I was to spend at least a quarter of an hour in their company I cannot, to this day, recollect a single feature or physical characteristic of either of them.

The next minute I was standing beside the man lying on the ground. It was one of our native soldiers, and I could tell by his build and features that he was a Zulu. As a Government official in Natal for some years, I had got to know this Bantu race, their language and customs well. A shell must have burst near him. His left arm was off at the elbow. A large splinter must have snapped it off as one snaps crisply and cleanly between one's fingers a sun-dried mealie stalk. His shirt, I noticed, was full of little craters, stiff with caked blood.

Then I saw his eyes. They were a luminous jet black, stricken
with pain; yet they seemed, somehow, detached. Although the
man was looking straight at me he appeared unaware of my
presence.

'*Kuyini umfana?* (What is it, young Zulu?)' I asked, bending
over him and hearing my voice go trailing over the sand with a
gruff undertone as if there were yet another imbecility for which I
wasn't in the least responsible and I resented being implicated in
it; as if what that droning voice really wanted to say was: 'I'm out
of it, do you hear? Out of it . . . Leave me alone! Why drag me
back? Why—'

Hearing his own language, the young Zulu raised his head
slightly. His eyes seemed brighter, but their expression had
changed; it was no longer remote, had become intimate. Then his
head fell back, his eyes, however, never leaving my face. '*Hau . . .
umlungu . . .*' he groaned. '*Kuhi . . . Insimbi Ingshayili . . .* (O . . .
white man . . . It is not a good thing . . . The iron has hit me . . .)'

Suddenly I realized I was normal again, with my mind no longer
split into segments, but an integrated whole with perfectly logical
perceptions and reactions.

I had come erect, was looking around. The German officer had
gone. About four hundred yards away I saw him, driving away in
his truck. I turned to the Zulu again. He was in a half-sitting
position with one of the two men who had stepped out of our lines
with me, crouched down behind him, holding him up.

'How do you feel, *umfana*?' I asked, going down on my right
knee. A hard glitter came into his eyes, then he said slowly,
clearly: '*Umlungu, ngidubule* . . . (White man, shoot me . . .)'
There was no doubting it, he was pleading with me—apparently
unaware that I, like him, was now a prisoner no longer carrying a
weapon and therefore as powerless as he against his fate.

'Don't talk like that, *umfana*,' I said peremptorily, more to get a
grip on myself than to rebuke him. 'You've only lost an arm.
Many men have lost an arm, and they're walking about now,
laughing, with their heads in the sun.'

'*Ca . . . ca . . .* (No . . . no . . .)' he muttered, almost angrily,
through tightly clenched teeth.

'Yes, yes . . .' I continued, speaking fast. 'We'll get a doctor for
you and we'll take you to the hospital'—we, we, who the hell's we,
I thought, we're nothing, less than nothing—'and they'll be good to
you there, soon you'll be a whole man again and it won't be many

moons before you'll be going about your work, watching the pumpkins fill out, the maize swell in the cob, and the cattle grow fat in the fields back in Zululand . . .'

I do not know what made me say this. I knew it wasn't true. My own words, with a hollow false sound, echoed back on my ears.

'*Ca, umlungu . . . Ngidubule! Ngidubule!* (No, white man . . . Shoot me! Shoot me!)' How strong his voice is, I thought, out of all proportion to his strength.

'Soon,' I repeated, 'you'll be a whole man again.'

'No, no, white man . . .' He was shaking his head in exactly the way I had so often seen old Zulu indunas shake their heads, when in tribal councils they would, by their whole expression and attitude, gently but firmly convey to the European that the sum of all his knowledge was as nothing compared with their ancient African wisdom. '*Ngipelile* . . . (I am finished . . .)'

A little desert car drew up twenty yards away. A tall, thin German officer with sharp features jumped out and was beside us in a few quick darting steps. Another German officer, short and squat, had followed him—and the next moment the tall officer was bending over the native, feeling his chest beneath the blood-stiffened shirt. Noticing his stars and the snake of Aesculapius in his badge, I felt at once greatly relieved.

I looked at the Zulu's arm again. Most of the stump's end was caked over with dry, hardened blood. It still bled, but very little, only a trickle oozing through the shattered flesh.

'*Ngidubule!*' His voice was no longer supplicating but had a fierce, ringing quality as if raised in protest that this was no extravagant demand but a fitting and just claim upon me. My gaze travelled over his magnificent body. The broad torso bulged beneath the army shirt. The thighs, curving into sight under the dirty bloodstained shorts, were of a classic symmetry, the calves and legs as harmoniously proportionate.

Then the thought struck me that the Zulus, physically, are one of the most beautiful races in the world; that Zulu males have an extraordinary pride in their physique; that they consider any deformity of the body—and particularly disfigurement—as something unnatural, even monstrous; and that formerly they killed all children unfortunate enough to be born cripples. Naturally this young Zulu, descended from generations of warriors, wanted to die now, clamoured for death; for this cracked useless body, this stump of an arm, were they not a shame and a disgrace, a crying offence against both man and the gods?

My eyes slipped over his chest again, met his. I knew they had never left my face even though the German doctor was still bending over him, examining him, feeling tentatively for his wounds. Now, quite simply, as if he had read my thoughts and was confident that his wish would be granted, he said slowly: '*Ngidubule, umlungu* . . .'

'No, you speak foolish things.'

'*Ngidubule!*' The short spell of calm had broken, the voice was again urgent. Did it contain a note of reproach?

'*Ngidubule, umlungu, ngidubule!*' Yes, it was reproachful. God, would that eternal cry of '*Ngidubule* . . .' never stop?

The doctor had pulled out his hand, turned and was looking at me.

'What does he say?' he asked me in German.

'It is his request that we shoot him . . .' I answered, realizing at once that I was giving a stiff literal German translation not of what the Zulu had said but of what his headman would have said in slow solemn tone to the other assembled members of the tribe were they here now, squatting in a half circle round the dying man, deliberating his case.

Whether the Zulu finally understood that I could not, would not do it, or whether he recognized the German doctor as his enemy who, according to his subconscious reasoning, would be less averse to such an action, I do not know; but as soon as he had heard this new, foreign voice intruding upon our dialogue, he was no longer looking at me but at the German.

Leaning up against the South African supporting him from behind, he had had until now his right hand on the ground. But now, in a great effort, his lips twitching in pain—there were foam flecks on them, spotted with blood—he brought his hand to his shirt front and slowly, gropingly, uncovered his chest. Next, straining himself forward, he said in a deep resonant voice to the German captain: '*Wena aungidubule!*' (You shoot me!) Strange, but at that moment it sounded almost like a command.

'He wants *you* to shoot him . . .' I told the doctor. Standing stiffly beside me, the German made no reply.

'What chance has he of living?' I asked.

'None,' came the incisive answer. 'He must have been wounded yesterday afternoon, has lain here all night. He's lost so much blood, he can't have much more to lose. Had he been a European he would have been dead long ago . . .' His voice was as jerky as his movements. Though speaking German, we had instinctively moved a few paces away as if afraid the wounded man would understand.

'And he still speaks,' the voice staccatoed on, 'with all that shrapnel inside him! He'll probably die when we move him. Then again, he's so strong he might live for hours.'

I turned to the native. 'The doctor says you are badly hurt, but that you have great strength and must not worry. We're going to carry you to that truck, take you to the hospital.'

'No, no . . . I am finished . . . Shoot me . . . I cannot live any more. The pain is too deep . . . *umlungu* . . .' He was groaning again, his voice getting weaker, and for the first time he closed his eyes for longer than a second. His hand, too, had fallen back on the ground, black against the pale yellow earth.

The doctor touched me on the arm. 'Perhaps it would be the easiest way out,' he said, and motioned to the young lieutenant standing a few paces away. An order from the captain, and the lieutenant had pulled out his pistol and handed it to me. I stood there, as if petrified, with the pistol in my right hand.

'*Umlungu . . . umlungu . . .*' were the only two words now uttered by the Zulu lying at my feet with closed eyes and quivering lips. He kept on muttering them, his voice never rising above a whisper. Yet the repeated '*umlungu . . . umlungu . . .*' seemed to contain a note of awe, almost of reverence—not, I felt, because I was an officer and he a private, but because at that moment I must have appeared to his bewildered mind, half crazed with pain, the great benefactor bearing in my hands the supreme gift of peace and the healing oblivion of death.

I looked from the pistol to the captain, from the captain back to the pistol, then at the Zulu. He, in the meanwhile, had opened his eyes.

'*Ngidubule!*' his voice rang in my ears, as strong as ever.

I shook my head. 'No,' I said to the captain, handing him the pistol, 'I do not shoot my friends.'

It was at least two seconds before I realized I had addressed the German in Zulu.

The Zulu's gaze had followed the motion of the pistol; he now stared at the captain. The German stood, irresolute, as if embarrassed by the pistol. He seemed to be debating a point. Then, turning to me, he said:

'My business is to preserve life not to destroy it.'

'And not to lessen pain?'

'Yes, to lessen pain.' He was speaking much more slowly; the bark had gone out of his voice. 'But that would be contrary to Red Cross regulations. I'm not even allowed to carry firearms . . .' This typical German respect for rules and regulations, I thought, how incongruous!

The next moment the captain had handed the pistol back to its owner. 'Herr Oberleutnant Müller,' he rapped out in military tone: 'Shoot this man!'

Then I noticed the Zulu's hand come creeping up his chest again and I forgot everything, watching it, fascinated. It was a broad compact hand with a fair-sized wart on the index finger and at that moment it seemed to pulse with life, to be one of the most living things I had ever seen. The big strong fingers felt for the edge of the shirt-front where the V-opening ended, closed it in a firm grip; there was the quick, sharp rip of khaki drill tearing, and the shirt fell apart, revealing the entire chest. The right side had hardly been touched but the left, until now concealed by the shirt, was a mass of torn flesh.

I looked away. The lieutenant had stepped forward, was standing a few feet from the Zulu. He had a set look on his face, holding the weapon stiffly in front of him, pointing it at the dying man.

The Zulu's hand was buried deep in the sand, gripping the earth, supporting his body. To me, at that moment, it seemed that in a last superhuman effort he wanted to lift himself, rise and, with both feet planted firmly on the ground, meet his death face to face. He had squared his shoulders, throwing them back, and was straining his chest out and up, as if to present a better target to the enemy, or to thrust it against the very muzzle of the pistol.

Now his eyes were ablaze, as if all the fierce passionate life that remained to him were concentrated in their jet-black depths.

'*Ngidubule! Ngidubule!*' broke from his dry, cracked lips in a crescendo, like a shout of joy, a triumphant roar; and I was reminded of the Zulu battle cry I had so often heard, sonorous and barbaric, bursting from a thousand throats when the war dance reaches its frenzied, crashing climax.

'*Ngidubule! Ngidubule!*'

Yes, he was roaring at his body, roaring at his pain, roaring at death.

Rooted to the spot, I stood looking down at him. I wanted to tear myself away. I couldn't.

Carefully, methodically, the lieutenant took aim along the pistol barrel.

I felt a hand clutch my shoulder. For a second it lay there, lax.

Then it tightened over my collarbone. I half turned. It was the captain. Slowly he turned me completely round. He took a step forward. I followed. I was waiting, I felt, for yet another '*Ngidubule!*' rather than the pistol's report; and when a snail-shell (one of those countless bone-white shells scattered like tiny skulls about the desert) popped under my feet, I shuddered.

We were about fifteen feet away when the pistol cracked. It did not go off again.

I have a very hazy recollection of what happened after that.

I remember the German captain saying, '*Auf wiedersehen*'; the two officers driving off in the small car; and that for a long time I sat on a flat stone beside the road.

Legs, many legs, milled past, kept slipping in and out of my vision. But they made no impression on me; in a dull, disconnected way I was more interested in the little wisps of sand that kept spiralling, circling about my boots and then settling in a thin, pale yellow dust on the broad square toe-caps.

How long I sat there, staring at my boots, I don't know. Someone shouted in Afrikaans: 'Come along, Du Toit! Come along!' and when I found myself again, I was once more among that crowd of prisoners tramping slowly, wearily towards Tobruk.

Alun Lewis

They Came

The evening was slowly curdling the sky as the soldier trudged the last mile along the lane leading from the station to the Hampshire village where he was billeted. The hedgerows drew together in the dusk and the distance, bending their waving heads to each other as the fawn bird and the black bird sang among the green hollies. The village lay merged in the soft seaward slope to the South Downs; the soldier shifted his rifle from left to right shoulder and rubbed his matted eyelashes with his knuckles. He was a young chap but, hampered by his heavy greatcoat and equipment, he dragged his legs like an old clerk going home late. He cleared his throat of all that the train journey, cigarettes and chocolate and tea and waiting had secreted in his mouth. He spat the thick saliva out. It hung on a twig.

Someone was following him. When he heard the footsteps first he had hurried, annoyed by the interfering sound. But his kit was too clumsy to hurry in and he was too tired. So he dawdled, giving his pursuer a chance to pass him. But the footsteps stayed behind, keeping a mocking interval. He couldn't stop listening to them, but he refused to look back. He became slowly angry with himself for letting them occupy his mind and possess his attention. After a while they seemed to come trotting out of the past in him, out of the Welsh mining village, the colliers gambling in the quarry, the country school where he learned of sex and of knowledge, and college where he had swotted and slacked in poverty, and boozed, and quarrelled in love. They were the footsteps of the heavy-jawed deacon of Zion, with his white grocer's apron and his hairy nostrils sniffing out corruption.

But that was silly, he knew. Too tired to control his mind, that's what it was. These footsteps were natural and English, the postman's perhaps . . . But still they followed him, and the dark gods wrestling in him in the mining valley pricked their goaty ears at sound of the pimping feet.

He turned the corner into the village and went down the narrow street past the post office and the smithy, turned the corner under the A.A. sign and crossed the cobbled yard of the hotel where the officers' and businessmen's cars were parked. A shaggy old dog came frisking out of its strawfilled barrel in the corner, jumping and barking. He spoke to it and at once it grovelled on its belly. He always played with the dog in the mornings, between parades. The unit did its squad drill in the hotel yard, kitchen maids watching flirtatiously through the windows, giggling, and the lavatory smelling either of disinfectant or urine.

He pushed open the little door in the big sliding doors of the garage which had been converted into a barrack room for the duration. Thin electric bulbs high in the cold roof dangled a weak light from the end of the twisted, wavering flex. Grey blankets folded over biscuits or straw palliasses down both sides of the room. Equipment hanging from nails on the whitewashed wall—in one corner a crucifix, over the thin, chaste, taciturn Irish boy's bed. He was the only one in the room, sitting on his bed in the cold dark corner writing in his diary. He looked up and smiled politely, self-effacingly, said 'Hello. Had a good leave?' and bent his narrow head again to read what he had written.

'Yes, thanks,' said the soldier, 'except for raids. The first night I was home he raided us for three hours, the sod,' he said, unbuckling his bayonet belt and slipping his whole kit off his shoulders.

Last time he returned from leave, four months back, he had sat down on his bed and written to his wife. They had married on the first day of that leave and slept together for six nights. This time he didn't ferret in his kitbag for notepaper and pencil. He went straight out.

The hotel management had set a room aside for the soldiers to booze in. It was a good class hotel, richly and vulgarly furnished with plush and mirrors and dwarf palms in green boxes. The auctioneers and lawyers and city men, the fishermen and golfers and bank managers, most of whom had weekend cottages or villas of retirement in commanding positions at the local beauty spots, spent the evening in the saloon bar and lounge, soaking and joking. So the soldiers were given a bare little bar parlour at the back, with a fire and a dartboard and two sawdust spitoons. The soldiers were glad of it. It was their own. They invited some of their pals from the village to play darts with them—the cobbler, the old dad who lived by himself in the church cottage and never shaved or washed, the poacher who brought them a plucked pheasant under his old coat sometimes—all the ones the soldiers liked popped in for an evening. A few girls, too, before the dance in the church hall, on Tuesdays.

Fred Garstang, from Portsmouth, and Ben Bryant, from Coventry, the two oldest soldiers in the unit—regulars who had never earned a stripe—were playing darts, two empty pint glasses on the mantelpiece by the chalk and duster.

"Owdee, Taffy?' they said in unison. "Ave a good leave, lad?'

'Yes, thanks,' he said automatically, 'except for raids. The sod raided us for three hours the first night I was home.'

'Damn. Just the wrong side of it,' said Fred, examining the quivering dart. 'I deserve to lose this bloody game, Ben. I 'xpect you're the same as me, Taff; glad to get back to a bit of peace and quiet and a good sleep. My seven days in Pompey's the worst I've ever spent in India, China, the Rhineland, Gallygurchy or anywhere. But we're nice and cosy here, thank God. They can keep their leave, *I* don't want seven nights in an Anderson. I'd rather stay here, I would.'

Old Fred never stopped talking once he started. The soldier tapped the counter with a shilling and leaned over to see whether the barmaid was on the other side of the partition. He saw her silky legs and the flutter of her skirt. He hit the counter harder, then, while he waited, wondered at his impatience. His body wasn't thirsty; it was too damned tired to bother, too worn-out. It was something else in him that wanted to get drunk, dead, dead drunk.

The barmaid came along, smiling. She was natural with the soldiers. She smiled when she saw who it was and held her pretty clenched fist to him across the counter. He should have taken it and forced it gently open, of course. Instead, he just put his flat palm underneath it. She looked at him with a hurt-faun reproach in her sailing eyes, and opening her hand let a toffee fall into his.

'One from the wood, Madge,' he said.

'I'll have to charge you for *that*,' she said.

'That's all right,' he replied. 'You always pay in this life.'

'Why don't you take the girl, Taffy?' said old Fred as he came and sat by them, their darts over. 'If I was your age—'

He had been in the army since he was fifteen. Now he was past soldiering, wandering in the head sometimes, doing odd jobs; in peace-time he kept the lawns trimmed at the depot, now he was tin-man in the cooking-shed, cleaning with Vim the pots and pans Ben Bryant used for cooking. 'Vermicelli tastes all right,' he said. 'Better than anything you can pick up in the streets. Yellow or black or white, German or Irish. I've never had a Russian though, never. It's not bad when you're young, like a new crane when the jib runs out nice and smooth; it's better than sitting in the trenches like an old monkey, scratching yourself and not knowing whose leg it is or whose arm it is, looking in his pockets to see if there's anything worth taking, and not knowing who'll win the race, the bullet with your number on it or the leaky rod you're nursing. But I like it here. It's nice and peaceful up here, in the cookhouse all day. We ought to try some vermicelli, Ben, one day.'

'Don't you get impatient now, Freddy,' Ben said with the calmness of a father of many children. 'We'll stuff your pillow full of it next Christmas and put a sprig of it on your chest. Don't you worry, boy.'

But old Fred went on talking like an old prophet in a volcanic world, about and about. 'There's no knowing when you've got to fight for your king and country,' he said. 'No matter who you are, Russian or Frenchy or Jerry—and the Yankee, too. He'll be in it. boy. I've seen him die. It's only natural, to my way of thinking. I wore a pair of gloves the Queen knitted herself, she did, last time. The Unknown Soldier I was, last time.'

None of us are ourselves now, the Welsh boy sat thinking: neither what we were, nor what we will be. He drained his pint glass and crossed to the counter, to Madge smiling there.

'You never looked round all the way up from the station,' she said, pulling her shoulder-straps up under her grey jumper and exposing the white rich flesh above her breasts.

'So it was you followed me, eh?' he said, sardonic.

'Why didn't you turn round?' she asked. 'Did you know it was me? You knew someone was behind you, I could tell.'

'I didn't turn round because I didn't want to look *back*,' he said.

'And you mean to say you don't know how the Hebrew puts out the eyes of a goldfinch?' Freddy's aggrieved voice swirled up.

'Afraid of being homesick for your wife, eh?' she jeered.

He covered his eyes with his hand, tired out, and looked up at the vague sensual woman playing upon his instincts there like a gipsy on a zither.

'Not homesick,' he said drily. 'Death-sick.'

'What d'you mean?' she said.

'Well, she was killed in a raid,' he shouted.

He went up to the orderly room then, having forgotten to hand in his leave pass to the orderly corporal. The room was in the corner of an old warehouse. The building also housed the kitchen

and the quartermaster's stores. About the high bare rooms with
their rotten dry floors and musty walls rats galloped in the darkness; in the morning their dirt lay fresh on the mildewed sacks and
the unit's cat stretched her white paws and got a weak and lazy
thrill from sniffing it.

The orderly corporal was dozing over a Western novelette from
Woolworth's, hunched up in a pool of lamp-and-fire-light.

'Hallo, Taffy,' he said. 'Had a good leave?'

'Yes thanks,' he replied. 'Except for raids. Am I on duty to-
morrow?'

'You're on duty tonight, I'm afraid,' the orderly corporal replied with the unctuous mock-regret of one who enjoys detailing
tired or refractory men for unexpected jobs. 'Dave Finley had a
cold on his chest this morning and didn't get out of bed. So they
fetched him out on a stretcher and the M.O. gave him pneumonia
pills before Dave could stop him; so he's got pneumonia now.
You'll go on guard at midnight and at six hours.'

'O.K.'

He turned to go.

'Better get some sleep,' said the orderly corporal, yawning
noisily. 'Hell! I'm browned off with this war.'

The soldier yawned too, and laughed, and returned to the
barrack room to lie down for a couple of hours. He rolled his
blankets down on the floor and stretched out.

Old Ben and Fred were back, also, Ben fixing bachelor buttons
into his best trousers and singing Nelly Dean comfortably to
himself, Fred muttering by the stove. 'There's some mean and
hungry lads in this room,' he said; 'very hungry and mean. It's an
awful nature, that. They'll borrow off you all right, but they won't
lend you the turd off their soles. And always swanking in the
mirror and talking all the time, saying Yes, they can do the job
easy. The fools! Whip 'em! Whip 'em!'

Ben was toasting bread on the point of his bayonet and boiling
water in his billy. A tin of pilchards left over from tea was for them
all.

'Come on, Taffy. Have a bellyful while you can,' he said.

'No thanks,' said the soldier, restless on his blankets. 'I don't
feel like food tonight, Ben, thanks.'

'Ain't you never bin hungry?' Fred shouted angrily. 'You don't
know what food is, you youngsters don't.'

'I've been without food,' the soldier said, thinking of the '26
strike; and going without peas and chips in the chip shop by the

town clock in college when a new book must be bought. But not now, when everything is free but freedom, and the doctor and dentist and cobbler send you no bills.

What survives I don't know, the soldier thought, rubbing his hot eyelids and shifting his legs on the spread-out blankets. What is it that survives?

He got up and buckled his battle order together, adjusting his straps, slipping the pull-through through his Enfield, polishing boots and buttons, tightening his helmet strap under his chin.

'There was a religious woman used to come to our house,' Ben was saying, 'and one day she said to me, sociable like, "You're a Guiness drinker, aren't you, Mr Bryant?" and I says "I am, mum," and she says "Well, can you tell me what's wrong with the ostrich on them advertisements?" '

The soldier went out to relieve the guard.

They were only twenty soldiers altogether, sent up here to guard a transmitting station hidden in the slopes of the Downs. A cushy job, safe as houses. There was a little stone shed, once used for sheep that were sick after lambing, in a chalky hollow on the forehead of the hill, which the guard used for sleeping in when they were off duty. Two hours on, four hours off, rain and sun and snow and stars. As the soldier toiled up the lane and across the high meadow to the shed, the milky moon came out from grey clouds and touched with lucid fingers the chopped branches piled in precise lengths at the foot of the wood. The pine trees moved softly as the moon touched their grey-green leaves, giving them a veil that looked like rainy snow, grey-white.

The lane running up through the wood shortened alarmingly in perspective. A star fell. So surprising, so swift and delicate, the sudden short curved fall and extinction of the tiny lit world. But over it the Plough still stayed, like something imperishable in man. He leant against the gate, dizzy and light-headed, waves of soft heat running into his head. He swallowed something warm and thick; spitting it out, he saw it was blood. He stayed there a little, resting, and then went on.

He went along the sandy lane, noticing as he always did the antique sculptures of sea and ice and rain, the smooth twisted flints, yellow and blue and mottled, lying in the white sand down which the water of winter scooped its way.

At the top of the lane was the lambing shed—guard room. He slipped quickly through the door to prevent any light escaping. There was gun-fire and the sound of bombs along the coast.

The sergeant of the guard was lying on a palliasse in front of the stove. He got up slowly, groaning lazily. 'So you're back again, Taffy, are you?' he said, a grudge in his too hearty welcome. 'Relieving Dave Finley, eh? He's swinging the lead, Dave is. I've a good mind to report him to the O.C. It's tough on you, going on night guard after a day's journey. Have a good leave, Taff?'

'Not bad,' the soldier replied, 'except for the raids. Raided us the first night I was home.'

'It's a sod, everybody's getting it,' the sergeant replied, yawning. 'They dropped two dozen incendiaries in our fields in Lincs, last week.'

He was drinking a billy can of cocoa which he had boiled on the fire, but he didn't offer any. He had weak blue eyes, a receding chin, fresh features of characterless good-looks, wavy hair carefully combed and brilliantined. He was always on edge against Taffy, distrusting him, perhaps envying him. He lived in terror of losing a stripe and in constant hunger to gain another promotion. He sucked and scraped the officers for this, zealously carrying out their orders with the finnicky short temper of a weak house-proud woman. He polished the barrack room floor and blackleaded the stove himself because the boys refused to do more than give the place a regulation lick. And he leaped at the chance of putting a man on the peg, he was always waiting to catch somebody cutting a church parade or nipping out of camp to meet a girl when he should be on duty. Yet he was mortally afraid of a quarrel, of unpopularity, and he was always jovial, glassily jovial, even to the Welsh boy whom he knew he couldn't deceive.

'Who am I to relieve on guard?' the soldier asked.

'Nobby Sherraton. He's patrolling the ridge.'

'O.K.' He slipped his rifle sling over his shoulder and put his helmet on. 'You marching me out? Or shall I just go and send Nobby in?'

For once laziness overcame discretion.

'There's nobody about. Just go yourself,' the sergeant said, smiling, posing now as the informal honest soldier. 'I'll be seeing yer.'

'Some day.'

He left the hut and crossed the dry dead-white grass to the ridge where Nobby was on guard.

Nobby was his mate.

He had only been in the unit about a month. Before that he had been stationed just outside London and had done a lot of demolition and rescue work. He was from Mile End, and had roughed it. His hands and face showed that, his rough blackened hands, cigarette-stained, his red blotchy face with the bulbous nose, and the good blue eyes under tiny lids, and short scraggy lashes and brows. His hair was mousy and thin. He had been on the dole most of the time. He had been an unsuccessful boxer; he cleared out of that game when his brother, also a boxer, became punch-drunk and blind. He had plenty of tales of the Mosley faction. He was sometimes paid five bob to break up their meetings. He always took his five bob but he let the others do the breaking up. Who wants a black eye and a cut face for five bob? 'Tain't worth it. He rarely said anything about women. He didn't think much of lots of them; though like all Cockney youths he loved the 'old lady', his mother. He wasn't married. No, sir.

He was a conscript. Naturally. He didn't believe in volunteering. And he didn't like the Army, its drills and orders and its insistence on a smart appearance. Smartness he disliked. Appearances he distrusted. Orders he resented. He was 'wise' to things. No sucker.

Taffy felt a warm little feeling under his skin, relief more than anything else, to see Nobby again. He hadn't to pretend with Nobby. Fundamentally they shared the same humanity, the unspoken humanity of comradeship, of living together, sharing what they had, not afraid to borrow or talk or shut up. Or to leave each other and stroll off to satisfy the need for loneliness.

Nobby was surprised so much that he flung out his delight in a shout and a laugh and a wave of his arms. 'Taffy, lad!' he said. 'Back already, eh? Boy!' Then he became normal.

'Can't keep away from this bloody sannytorium for long, can we?' he grumbled.

Taffy stood looking at him, then at the ground, then he turned away and looked nowhere.

'What's wrong, kid?' Nobby said, his voice urgent and frightened, guessing. 'Anything bad? Caught a packet, did you?' He said the last two phrases slowly, his voice afraid to ask.

'*I* didn't,' Taffy said, his voice thin and unsteady. '*I* didn't. *I'm* all right. *I'm* healthy.'

Nobby put his hand on his shoulder and turned him round. He looked at the white sucked-in face and the eyes looking nowhere.

'Did *she* get it?' and he too turned his head a little and swallowed. 'She did,' he said, neither asking a question nor making a statement. Something absolute, the two words he said.

Taffy sat down, stretched out. The grass was dead; white, wispy long grass; Nobby sat down, too.

'They came over about eight o'clock the first night,' Taffy said. 'The town hadn't had a real one before. I've told you we've only got apartments, the top rooms in an old couple's house. The old ones got hysterics, see, Nobby. And then they wouldn't do what I told them, get down the road to a shelter. They wouldn't go out into the street and they wouldn't stay where they were. "My chickens," the old man was blubbering all the time. He's got an allotment up on the voel, see? Gwyneth made them some tea. She was fine, she calmed them down. That was at the beginning, before the heavy stuff began. I went out the back to tackle the incendiaries. The boy next door was out there, too. He had a shovel and I fetched a saucepan. But it was freezing, and we couldn't dig the earth up quick enough. There were too many incendiaries. One fell on the roof and stuck in the troughing. The kid shinned up the pipe. It exploded in his face and he fell down. Twenty odd feet. I picked him up and both his eyes were out, see?'

He had gone back to the sing-song rhythm and the broad accent of his home, the back lanes and the back gardens. He was shuddering a little, and sick-white, sallow.

Nobby waited.

'I took him into his own house,' he said, controlling his voice now, almost reflective. 'I left him to his sister, poor kid. Then I went to see if Gwyneth was all right. She was going to take the old couple down the road to the shelter. She had a mack on over her dressing gown. We'd intended going to bed early, see? So I said she was to stay in the shelter. But she wanted to come back. We could lie under the bed together.

'I wanted her back, too, somehow. Then some more incendiaries fell, so I said "Do as you like" and went at them with a saucepan. I thought sure one would blow my eyes out. Well, she took them down. Carried their cat for them. Soon as she'd gone the heavy stuff came. Oh Christ!'

Nobby let him go on; better let him go on.

'It knocked me flat, dazed me for a bit. Then I got up and another one flattened me. It was trying to stop me, see, Nobby. I crawled out of the garden, but it was dark as hell and buildings all down, dust and piles of masonry. Then he dropped some more incendiaries and the fires started. I knew she must be somewhere, see? I knew she must be somewhere. I began pulling the masonry away with my hands, climbed on to the pile of it in the fire. I couldn't see with the smoke and I knew it wasn't any use, only I had to do it, see?

'Then suddenly the masonry fell downwards. The road was clear on the other side. I thought it was all right after all, then. I thought she'd have reached the shelter . . . But she hadn't.

'I found her about twenty yards down the road.

'She wasn't dead. Her clothes were gone. And her hands. She put them over her face, I reckon.

'She couldn't speak, but I knew she knew it was me.

'I carried her back in my arms. Over the fallen house. The fire wasn't bad by then. Took her home, see, Nobby. Only the home was on fire. I wanted her to die all the time. I carried her over a mile through the streets. Fires and hoses and water. And she wouldn't die. When I got her to the clearing station I began to think she'd live.

'But they were only playing a game with me, see?'

He stood up and made himself calm.

'Well, there it is,' He rubbed his face with the palm of his hand, wiping the cold sweat off.

'I knew she was going to die. When they told me she was—I didn't feel anything, Nobby.

'But she died while they were messing her body about with their hands, see?

'And she never said anything. Never said anything to me.

'Not that it makes any difference, I suppose. We never did speak about those things much. Only, you know how it is, you want a word somehow. You want it to keep.'

'Sure. I know,' Nobby said.

'What's it all for, Nobby?' he said in a while. He looked so tired and beat. 'I used to know what it was all about, but I can't understand it now.'

'Aw, forget all about that,' Nobby said. 'You're here aincher, now?'

He put his hands on his mate's shoulders and let him lean against him for a bit.

'I reckon you belong to each other for keeps, now,' Nobby said.

'You believe that, Nobby?' he asked, slow and puzzled, but with a gathering force as his uncertainty came together.

'Yes. For you and 'er, I do. It wouldn't be true for me, or the sergeant in there, but for you two it is.'

Taffy was still against his shoulder. Then slowly he straightened himself, moved back on to himself, and lifting his face he looked at the milky-white fields and the sentinel pines and the stars.

'I knew it was so, really,' he said. 'Only I was afraid I was fooling myself.'

He smiled, and moved his feet, pressing on them with his whole weight as if testing them after an illness.

'I'm all right now, Nobby. Thank you, boy.'

'I'll go then,' Nobby said. He slipped his rifle over his shoulder and as he moved off he hesitated, turned back, and touched his mate's arm lightly.

'Two's company, three's none,' he said, and stumped off slowly to the lambing shed through the dead straw-grass.

And the soldier was left alone on the flat upland ridge.

Below him the valleys widened into rich arable lakes on which the moonlight and the mist lay like the skeins which spiders spin round their eggs. Beyond the pools another chain of downland lay across the valleys, and beyond those hills the coast. Over him, over the valleys, over the pinewoods, blue fingers came out of the earth and moved slanting across their quarters as the bombers droned in the stars over his head and swung round to attack the coastal city from inland. The sky over the coast was inflamed and violent, a soft blood-red.

The soldier was thinking of the day he received his calling up papers, just a year ago. Sitting on the dry-stone wall of his father's back garden with Gwyneth by him; his ragged little brother kneeling by the chicken-run, stuffing cabbage stumps through the netting for the hens to peck, and laughing and pulling the stumps out as the old hen made an angry jab; his father riddling the ashes and the ramshackle garden falling to bits, broken trellis and tottering fence; his mother washing her husband's flannel vest and drovers in the tub, white and vexed. He had taken Gwyneth's hand, and her hand had said, 'In coming and in going you are mine; now, and for a little while longer; and then for ever.'

But it was not her footsteps that followed him down the lane from the station.

Now over his head the darkness was in full leaf, drifted with the purity of pines, the calm and infinite darkness of an English night, with the stars moving in slow declension down the sky. And the warm scent of resin about him and of birds and of all small creatures moving in the loose mould in the ferns like fingers in velvet.

And the soldier stood under the pines, watching the night move down the valleys and lift itself seawards, hearing the sheep cough and farm-dogs restlessly barking in the farms. And farther still the violence growing in the sky till the coast was a turbulent thunder of fire and sickening explosions, and there was no darkness there at all, no sleep.

'My life belongs to the world,' he said. 'I will do what I can.'

He moved along the spur and looked down at the snow-grey ever-green woods and the glinting roofs scattered over the rich land.

And down in the valleys the church bells began pealing, pealing, and he laughed like a lover, seeing his beloved.

Liam O'Flaherty

The Alien Skull

When he was within ten yards of the enemy outpost, Private
Mulhall lay flat, with his right ear close to the ground. He listened
without drawing breath. He strained his ear to catch a word, a
cough, or the grating sound of a boot touching the frost-bound
earth. There was no sound.

Had they gone?

It was eleven o'clock at night. There was perfect silence along
that section of the battle-front. In the distance there was the
monotonous and melancholy murmur of heavy guns in action.
Here everything was still, as in a tomb. The moon had not risen.
But the sky was not dark. It was an angry blue colour. There were
stars. It was possible to see the ground for a long distance. It was
freezing heavily. Bayonets, lying beside dead men, gleamed. All
the huddled figures scattered about between the two lines of
trenches were dead men. There had been a battle that day.

They had sent out Mulhall to discover whether the enemy had
retired from his front line. If so, an advance was to be made at
midnight into the trenches evacuated by him. If possible, Mulhall
was to bring back a live prisoner. A man had been seen a little
earlier peering over the top of the advanced post, before which
Mulhall was now lying.

Irritated by the silence, Mulhall began to curse under his
breath. He had ceased to listen and looked back towards his own
line. He had come up a slope. He saw the dim shapes of the newly
made scattered posts, the rambling wire fences and the heaps of
rooted earth. He cursed and felt a savage hatred against his
officers. He had now been three years at the front without leave.
He was always doing punishment behind the line for insolence
and insubordination. In the line he was chosen for every danger-
ous duty, because of his ferocious courage. But as soon as he came
out he was up again before the adjutant, taken dirty on parade,
absent, drunk, or for striking a corporal.

Lying flat on the ground, Mulhall thought savagely of the
injustice done to him. He thought with cunning pleasure of crawl-

ing back towards his own line and shooting one of the officers or sergeants against whom he had a grudge. With pleasure, he rehearsed, in his mind, this act, until he saw the stricken victim fall, writhe, and lie still. Then terrible disciplinary cries rose up before his mind, his own name shouted by the sergeant, and then the giant figure of the sergeant-major, with his pace stick under his arm, heels together, erect, reading out the documentary evidence. A whole lot of shouting and stamping and awe-inspiring words. An enormous, invisible, inhuman machine, made of terrible words, constituted in his mind the terror that gave power to his superiors over him.

Compared to that it was pleasant out here.

He turned his head and looked towards the enemy outpost again. His hatred was now directed against the enemy. Their words were meaningless. Whenever he heard their words, they sounded like the barking of a dog. He was not afraid of them, and his punishment was remitted when he killed one or two of them.

Now he ceased to think and he thrust upwards his lower lip. His body became rigid. He fondled the breech of his rifle. With his rifle folded in his arms, ready for use, he slowly pushed his body forward, moving on his left side. He propelled himself with his left foot. He was listening intently. He moved like a snail, a few inches at a time. He made no sound. Then he stopped suddenly when he had gone half the distance. He had heard a sound. It was the sound of teeth gnawing a crust of hard bread, an army biscuit or a stale piece of bread, hardened by the frost. An enemy! There was an enemy there in front, five yards away.

He turned over gently on his stomach and brought his rifle to the front. Then he slowly touched various parts of his equipment and of his weapon to see that everything was in order. He settled his steel hat a little farther forward on his head, so that its rim shielded his face. Then he raised his back until he was on his elbows and knees. He then raised his feet and hands. He crawled forward as slowly as before and even more silently, breathing gently through his nose. He reached the post and lay still, behind a little knoll that formed the parapet. The enemy was within a yard of him. The enemy snuffled as he chewed at the crust.

Mulhall slowly raised his right knee. He put his right foot to the ground under him. He balanced his rifle in his right hand. He put his left hand on the ground. Then he jumped. He jumped right on top of the man in the hole beyond. But his foot struck something hard as he fell downwards and he tumbled over the man, losing his rifle. His head struck the side of the hole. He was slightly dazed. Almost immediately, however, he raised himself and held out his hands to grope for the enemy.

The enemy had also been tossed by the impact. Just then he was pulling himself up against the side of the hole, his hands supporting him, his mouth and eyes wide open with fright and wonder. There was a piece of black bread in his right hand. There were crumbs on his lips. His face was within a few inches of Mulhall's face.

Mulhall's hands, which he had thrust forward instinctively to grapple with the enemy, instinctively dropped. With the amazing courage of stupid men, Mulhall saw at a glance that the enemy was much bigger and stronger than himself and that he was almost standing up. Mulhall, on the other hand, was huddled on the ground. Now the enemy was incapable of movement through the paralysis of sudden fear. But if Mulhall touched him the same terror would make him struggle like a madman. Mulhall knew that and lay still. His face imitated the enemy's face. He opened his mouth and dilated his eyes.

They remained motionless, watching one another, like two strange babies. Their rifles lay side by side at the bottom of the hole. The enemy's rifle had been leaning against the side of the hole, and Mulhall had tripped over it, losing his own rifle. Now they were both unarmed. Their faces were so close together that they could hear one another's breathing.

The enemy was a stripling, but fully grown, and of a great size. His cheeks were red and soft. So were his lips. His whole body was covered with good, soft flesh. Mulhall was a squat fellow, thin and hard. His face was pale and marked with scars. He had eyes like a ferret. A drooping, fair moustache covered his lip and curled into his mouth. He looked brutal, ugly, war-worn and humpy compared to the fine young enemy, whose flesh was still soft and fresh on his big limbs.

Although his mouth lay stupidly open, as if with terror, Mulhall's mind remained brutal, calm, and determinedly watching for an opportunity to capture the enemy. If he could only reach his gun or disengage his entrenching tool or release his jack-knife. But he must take the fellow alive and drag him back over the frosty ground by the scruff of the neck, prodding him with his bayonet.

Then the enemy did a curious thing that completely puzzled Mulhall. At first his face broke into a smile. Then he laughed outright, showing his teeth that were sound and white, like the teeth of a negro. He made a low, gurgling sound when he laughed. Then, slowly, with a jerky, spasmodic movement, he raised the hand that held the crust until the bread was in front of Mulhall's face. Then his face became serious again and his expression changed.

The look of fear left his eyes. They became soft and friendly. His lips trembled. Then his whole body trembled. Gesticulating with his hands and shoulders, he offered the bread to Mulhall eagerly. He moved his lips and made guttural sounds which Mulhall did not understand. Every other time that Mulhall heard those words he thought they were like the barking of a dog. But now they had a different sound.

Mulhall became confused and ashamed. His forehead wrinkled. At first, he felt angry with the enemy, because he had aroused a long-buried feeling of softness. Then he became suspicious. Was the bread poisoned? No. The enemy had been eating it himself. Then he suddenly wanted to shed tears. He thought, with maudlin self-pity, of the brutal callousness and cruelty of his own comrades and superiors. Everybody despised Mulhall. Nobody would share blankets with him in the hut. He always got the dregs of the tea. They moved away from him in the canteen. When he was tied to the wheel of the cook-house cart fellows used to jeer at him and cry out: 'Are they bitin' ye, Mull?' With tears in his eyes, Mulhall wanted to bite the hand that held out the bread. The action brought to a climax the whole ghastly misery of his existence. It robbed him of his only solace, the power to hate somebody whom he could injure with impunity.

He was on the point of striking away the bread when his instinct of cunning warned him. So he took the bread. He fumbled with it uncertainly. Then he stuffed it into the pocket of his tunic. The enemy became delighted and made fresh gestures, gabbling all the while.

Then the enemy stopped gabbling and both became still, watching one another. Their faces became suspicious again. Their eyes wandered over one another's bodies, each strange to the other. Their features became hostile. Their hands jerked uneasily.

Mulhall, slightly unnerved by the enemy's action, began to feel afraid. He became acutely conscious of the enemy's size. So he also began to make guttural sounds imitating the enemy. He touched the enemy's sleeve and said: 'Huh. Yuh. Uh. Uh.' Then he put his finger in his mouth and sucked it. Then he nodded his head eagerly. The enemy looked on in wonder, with suspicion in his eyes.

Mulhall took off his steel hat. There was a crumpled cigarette in the hat. He took out the cigarette and gave it to the enemy.

The enemy's face relaxed again. He was overcome with emotion. He took the cigarette and then kissed Mulhall's hand.

Then Mulhall surrendered completely to this extraordinary new feeling of human love and kindness. Were it not for his native sense of reserve, he would return the enemy's kiss. Instead of that he smiled like a happy child and his head swam. He took the enemy's hand and pressed it three times, mumbling something inaudible. They sat in silence for a whole minute, looking at one another in a state of ecstasy. They loved one another for that minute, as saints love God or as lovers love, in the first discovery of their exalted passion. They were carried up from the silent and frightful corpse-strewn battle-field into some God-filled place, into that dream state where life almost reaches the secret of eternal beauty.

They were startled from their ecstasy by the booming of a single cannon, quite near, to the rear of the enemy lines. They heard the whizzing of the shell over their heads, flying afar.

The enemy soldier started. His face grew stern. He sat up on his heels and took Mulhall's hand. He began to make guttural sounds as he pressed Mulhall's hand fervently.

Mulhall also awoke, but slowly. His soul had sunk deeply into the tender reverie of human love so alien to him. Like a sick man awaking from a heavy sleep, he scanned the enemy's face, seeking the meaning of the change that had been caused by the boom and the whizzing passage of the shell. Slowly he became aware of the boom. Then his cunning awoke in him. Was it a signal?

Without changing his features he became cruel again.

Still uttering guttural sounds, the enemy crawled out into the bottom of the hole and picked up his rifle. Mulhall struggled between the desire of his cunning to throttle the enemy while his back was turned, and an almost identical desire to throw his arms around the enemy's neck and beg him to remain. The cunning desire lost in the struggle and he felt very lonely and miserable as if he were on the point of losing somebody he had loved all his life. So he remained motionless, watching the enemy with soft eyes. And yet he felt violently angry at not being able to hate the enemy and throttle him.

Having taken up his rifle, the enemy paused and looked at the crumpled cigarette which he still held in his hand. Then he smiled and began to make effusive gestures. He kissed the cigarette. Then he made curious sounds, his face aglow with joy and friendship. Then he put down his rifle, pointed to Mulhall's helmet and then to his own. He laughed. He took off his own helmet, which was shaped differently from Mulhall's helmet.

Immediately, Mulhall started violently. He became rigid. All his savagery and brutality again returned. The enemy's skull was exposed. As soon as he saw it the lust of blood overwhelmed him, as if he were a beast of prey in sight of his quarry. The enemy's bare skull acted on his senses like a maddening drug. Its shape was alien. It was shaped like a bullet. It had whitish hairs on it. It was hostile, foreign, uncouth, the mark of the beast. The sight of it caused his blood to curdle in him. A singing sound started in his head, at the rear of his forehead. His eyes glittered. He wanted to kill. He again felt exalted, gripped by the fury of despair.

The skull disappeared. The enemy put his helmet back on his head and then peered over the top of the hole in both directions. Then he struck his chest a great blow, murmured something, and crawled out back towards his own line.

As quick as a cat Mulhall pounced on his own rifle and arranged the breech. Then he crouched up against the side of the hole, thrust out his rifle and looked. The enemy was already a few yards away, slouching off in a stooping position. Quickly, taking quick aim, Mulhall fired. The enemy grunted, stopped, and expanded his chest. Then he turned his head towards Mulhall as he sank slowly. Baring his teeth, with glittering eye, Mulhall aimed slowly at the wondering, gaping young face of the enemy. He fired. The enemy's face twitched and lowered to the ground. His whole body lowered to the ground, trembled and lay still. The haunches remained high off the ground. The feet were drawn up. One hand was thrown out. The head was twisted around towards Mulhall. The face, now stained with blood, still seemed to look at Mulhall with awe and wonder.

Mulhall suddenly felt an irresistible desire to run away.

He dashed out of the hole in the direction of his own line, careless of taking cover. He had not gone three yards when he threw up his hands and dropped his gun. He got it right between the shoulder blades. Coughing and cursing, he fell backwards on his buttocks. His head was still erect. With maniacal joy he looked up into the cruel blue sky and laughed out fierce blasphemies.

They got him again, three times, around the shoulders and

neck. His head fell forward. In that position he lay still, like a grotesque statue, dead.

At dawn, when the sun began to shine, he was still sitting that way, like a Turk at prayer, stiff and covered with frost.

Wingult

There are few who can have encountered that extraordinary apparition, Wingult. He came on the scene in the first year of the Great War, and held the stage for a while, an uncouth hero of strange significance. He went his way as one who came from a far country and from a remote antiquity. He was like those legendary warriors and heroes of old, who performed the deeds of giants, and another age would easily have made of his doings a myth, whereby, quitting the men whom he served, he would have gone over to the gods.

Towards the end of the first great movements of the War, when the opposing armies were settling down into their two endless fronts, digging themselves into the earth and rock, to contest for months the possession of some scrap of land or little hillock, instead of trying for a decisive result, a singular fellow arrived in a French village with a small draft of reinforcements for a German squadron of dragoons. Like the others, he was leading his horse by the bridle, for they had detrained at a convenient distance from the front and had had a long way to go. The squadron commander, who had billeted his squadron in the village, came out of his courtyard on to the village street on the arrival of the new draft. He asked the men their names and ages.

'Wingult,' answered the singular one, when it came to his turn, 'thirty-five.'

The officer paused to look at the man. The fellow's neck was bent forward, he had gigantic shoulders and a powerful back, long arms and monstrous hands; resting, as though wedged into his strong legs, he suggested a bridge pier left behind when the rest of the bridge had been taken away. Slow, heavy movements revealed a superhuman strength.

'So you're a volunteer? When did you do your service? What's your profession?'

He had never been a soldier, Wingult answered.

'How's that?' asked the Captain. 'Why weren't you called up?'

Wingult grinned somewhat sheepishly, grasped at his back with one of his hands, and said: 'I didn't fit into a parade, I believe.'

That was true enough: a bridge pier like that was not easy to fit into a smart company marching in line.

Wingult was by trade a stevedore on the Rhine. The weights which he had been accustomed to load and unload had, no doubt, from an early age developed in his shoulders those layers of muscle which now made them look so prodigious. His mind was occupied with no other thought but to consider what could be achieved with the strength of one's body. Year in, year out, day in, day out, he had lifted ever heavier weights, bearing them upon the iron masses of his shoulders to the place where they belonged. He had grown to this service and indifferent to the efforts which it required. But he had grown proud that he was stronger than others.

The Captain asked whether he had taken the oath. Wingult did not know what this meant, and it was explained to him that it was the oath of allegiance to Emperor and Country. Wingult did not understand; he was only entering a service; he was doing his job for board and pay. It was explained to him that he had to swear to the Emperor, and Wingult asked whether the Emperor would also swear to him. As a precautionary measure he crossed himself, when, following the example of the others, he raised his hand to take the oath. Would that affect his having a job? He only wanted to do his job, he protested, having in mind a simple relationship which he understood and could appreciate. And he wanted a service book in which everything should be entered. This was promised him; he would have his paybook, and with that Wingult seemed to be satisfied.

Quite as a matter of course, as though it were automatically his job, Wingult proceeded to take on all the heavy duties in his squadron that he could. He groomed six horses instead of one; he carried the whole of the squadron's ration of oats from the cart; alone he shouldered the enormous heavy chests of clothing that arrived almost daily, hitching them into position on his neck without anyone having to lend a hand; and in the smithy he would snatch the legs of the most refractory horses from the ground, when they refused to be shoed, so that they never thought of kicking or lying down. But all this didn't count, and after a few days Wingult began to grieve that no scope was given for warlike deeds, or indeed for work of some other kind, such as would have brought his giant strength into play. The squadron was resting, and apart from routine, police, and fatigue duties there were no laurels to be won. Moreover, during this phase of the War, with its constantly reviving hopes of a big push or a break through, no one had decided what to do with the cavalry. When he had taken the few sacks from the ration cart and seen to his horses, Wingult would run around disconsolately like a veritable Atlas, who had been robbed of his globe and did not know what to do without his accustomed burden.

The first time after his arrival that he was on parade for kit inspection, it was noticed that he had attached a small round, almost spherical, stone bottle or jar with a short neck to his bayonet. The bottle was closed with a large greasy cork, and the mouth of the bottle had an oily gleam. He was ordered not to take the article with him, as it was not part of his equipment and would only get in the way. Two service flasks containing coffee or tea or whatever he might want were permissible.

Thoughtfully Wingult took the offending object back to his quarters and detached it; but at the next kit inspection he again appeared with the greasy stone jar on a strap. The sergeant, irritated at this disregard of orders, asked him what on earth was in the bottle. 'Petroleum,' answered Wingult. What was the good of that? the sergeant asked. Did he carry a lamp too? But Wingult replied that it was not for a lamp that he wanted the petroleum but for the fire-spitting mountain. The sergeant asked him angrily what on earth that was, but he was quite unable to get any explanation out of Wingult except that the petroleum was used for some trick. He needed it and it gave him pleasure. Others carried a mouth organ or something of the kind, and this was the same sort of thing. The other dragoons laughed at the simpleton's obstinacy and the insistence with which he fought for his hobby against the young N.C.O.; and as there could not be any question of Wingult's powerful limbs being burdened by such a small object he kept his stone jar.

As his days and nights passed in an inactivity which drew from Wingult more sighs than any weight which had ever pressed upon his back, he would clutch spasmodically at the mysterious jar that hung from his belt. It seemed as though he were considering a resolution to free himself decisively somehow. But he would always push the stone bottle back as though he had decided not to resort to extreme measures. One evening, however, he could restrain himself no longer. The other men although not so fidgety as Wingult, were sitting in weary boredom around a solitary candle in a large, empty inn parlour. 'Hi, you chaps,' he suddenly shouted to them—'watch the fire-spitting mountain.' There was a pause and Wingult crossed himself. Then he took an enormous pull at the jar and blew through the flame of a match which he had struck quickly on the palm of his hand. A heavy cloud of flame proceeded from his face and dissipated itself in tongues of fire running in all directions.

The dragoons, although they were pretty hardened old soldiers, leapt to their feet in surprise and alarm. The exhibition may have been Wingult's own invention or he may have picked it up from a stevedore on the Rhine, but none of them had seen it before. The air was hot and thick with the stink of burnt petrol. They all had a bitter, unpleasant taste in their mouths. Many of them were quite shaken and no one uttered a word. Wingult, however, roared in unrestrained ecstasy. He had been a success, and as he left he felt as Apollo may have done after transporting himself and the assembled gods with the harp. He had exercised great restraint in resorting to the consolations of the stone jar, as though he feared that repetition might cause it to lose virtue. The fire-spitting mountain was a last resource, a wild, fierce sacrament only to be invoked at the highest pitch of spiritual exacerbation. The first exhibition seemed to calm him for a few days, but this calm did not last long. 'Give me something to do and to eat,' he shouted, 'or I'll run away.' And he confirmed this threat with the most obscene and filthy oaths that have ever issued from the mouth of man. He felt he had been ordained to perform war-like deeds, and every evening he would report to the N.C.O. in charge, demanding his right as though it were a personal obligation of the latter. 'If it weren't for the Lieutenant I should have run away long ago,' said Wingult after these discussions, as he looked towards the front.

As Wingult spoke in such deadly earnest, and as he was truly formidable when he prowled restlessly about after finishing his work, which he polished off with the greatest ease, his remarks were reported to the squadron commander. The Captain tried to pacify him by pointing out that in the War each man had to remain at his post, and that Wingult would get his chance in due course. 'Yes, but I have not got a post,' Wingult replied. He had been told that war demanded extreme effort and he was disappointed at being given tasks which made no real call on his strength. 'I can do a great deal more,' he said plaintively, standing like a humble giant. Could he shoot straight? Had he had any training at the rifle range? the Captain asked, seeking for some way out. This question took Wingult by surprise. He had had that kind of casual training in the elementary use of a rifle which was all that was thought necessary before sending troops to the front, but he really despised it. Anyone could shoot; it had no attraction for him. 'If I can get near enough I don't need to shoot,' he said finally, after some hesitation.

He certainly would have run away had it not been for Salzach, the junior subaltern, who inspired in Wingult a curious and tender affection. Salzach was still in the first bloom of youth, and the schoolroom seemed a more appropriate place for him than the battlefield. His delicate build was ill-fitted to deal with the hard work of campaigning, and this made a special appeal to Wingult, who derived enormous satisfaction from such occasional services as he could render. He would groom the officer's horse from head to tail and put the saddle with all its equipment in place, which the young lad was never able to do alone. And in the evening he would always come to see that his officer had all the blankets he needed, for it was a cold time of the year, and if Wingult thought that the weather was too cold he would wrap the lad in a second rug of his own and go to sleep himself with nothing to cover him. All of what might be called love in that great rude soul was given to the subaltern, and it was in him alone that Wingult confided. Thus Salzach learned that Wingult had a woman at home on the Rhine with whom he seemed to run a household. They would always go up or down the Rhine on Sundays in a steamer. Never anywhere except on the Rhine, and that had been Wingult's conception of pleasure. But now he felt impelled to do deeds of heroism. He never got a letter from the woman and he never wrote himself; no doubt they would find writing too difficult. But once a month a hard black sausage arrived for Wingult. When Salzach offered to write a letter for him he declined, explaining that it was understood between them that everything was all right as long as the old woman sent the sausage.

In no way could Wingult more clearly have demonstrated his devotion to the subaltern than by the readiness with which he would offer to perform the dark rite to comfort him. When he saw his officer secretly weeping as he thought of his sisters at home and his brothers at the front, his spirit exhausted and broken by all the bitterness of the War, then Wingult would proceed to try to cheer him up by the well-known expedient that had never failed on himself. 'Sir,' he would say, looking at him sadly, and with all the tenderness that he could muster—'Sir, shall I do the fire-spitting mountain?' and he would beam at him. But Salzach, who

had been privileged to be present at the reeking ceremony when
Wingult first astonished his comrades with the performance, did
not share the belief in its beneficial effect upon his spirit and
declined. 'No, Wingult,' he would answer, not without emotion,
'We must not cheapen it.' He smiled, and Wingult would feel
comforted that by the mere mention of his precious turn he had
cheered the boy up.

After hanging round for a few more weeks the squadron was at
last ordered off with some other troops to the front. Wingult
became more cheerful. For the first few days certain clearing-up
operations were to be carried out over newly won territory;
afterwards the squadron was to be divided into two sections and
go into the trenches. Wingult threw himself into the work with a
foretaste of heroic deeds to come.

On this section of the front the Germans had made no incon-
siderable advance, and had won a good deal of new ground.
Young and inexperienced Canadian troops were endeavouring to
regain these positions, which enjoyed great natural advantages
and dominated a flat valley. Those were the memorable days
towards the end of May, which dealt havoc among the Canadian
Divisions. In bright daylight the Canadians went forward in close
formation to be greeted by countless greedy German machine-
guns, and to die blissfully like madmen, who know nothing of
death. New regiments followed one another, hour after hour, and
when night came the moon illuminated a sleeping host in front of
the German line, lying regularly man by man, never to wake
again. By the end of the following day, the enemy being unable to
offer any serious resistance, the Germans had advanced their line
to the low ground without any trouble, leaving the dead army
behind them. But by the fifth day the enemy dead were still
unburied, for new battles had taken place. The enemy trenches
were reversed, new strong points were formed, communication
trenches were dug, and what had been won almost without
bloodshed had now to be defended by hard fighting. One's own
dead and wounded needed every available man and stretcher.

As Wingult, walking by the side of the little subaltern, who was
in command of the section, moved into the wide shallowy valley,
he surveyed the battlefield with the eyes of a giant to whom alone
fell the duty of action. The moon was bright enough to reveal that,
even in the small section which had been allotted to the dragoons,
many hundreds of corpses were lying. These days of May, following upon many cold weeks, had been very hot. The nights were

oppressive. A ghastly miasma of putrefaction lay upon the field and stank to heaven. The men sweated at every pore; they almost fainted at the odour of dead bodies.

But the job had to be done and they set to work. It soon became obvious that it was impossible to give each man a separate grave, and those terrible graves were thrown up bearing the following legends: 'Here lie 8 Canadians; here lie 23 Canadians; here lie 45 Canadians; here lie 70 Canadians.' Wingult and those who had stretchers, or improvised them out of tent canvas, carried the corpses; the others dug. Wingult lifted his corpses alone, shouldered them crosswise, carried them across, and then let them slip over his powerful neck into the communal grave. He spoke not a word; he never looked up, sighed, or shuddered, giving each body to the earth as though he were working in the service of Death himself.

Thus two nights passed. No one would have ventured to show himself in the valley by day. Although on the second night those who had been out the night before were relieved, Wingult returned to his job. He slipped hundreds of corpses across his neck; his muscles were taut like twisted ropes, his breath came regularly, and he carried on in his businesslike way. By the end of that night they were all buried.

When he got back to his quarters next morning he went up to the subaltern, who was still fast asleep, exhausted by the first night's work. He let him rest, but before lying down himself he did the fire-spitting mountain all over the courtyard to commemorate the triumphant conclusion of his terrible handiwork. Then he watered the horses in the stable and lay down to sleep.

For some reason or other the entry of the dragoons into the trenches was delayed by a week. Wingult was craving for fresh deeds. His fellows laughed at him; they told him that at the front he would just have to sit down under the shells and the lice, and in any case he wasn't interested in rifle shooting. Only an attack would appeal to him. Wingult said he would find something to do all right. When at last the men chosen for the trenches—a certain number had to remain behind with the horses—arrived at the section allotted to them, they found that they were stationed on the edge of a flat, marshy piece of ground through which a slow stream ran. This stream had been almost completely dammed by the enemy by an oblique embankment, which they kept under constant fire, converting the ground into an impassable morass, although the water was not of any great depth except in the actual bed of the stream. Wingult surveyed the low ground, looking across the stretch of water, through which the tops of the tall reeds just appeared, at the rising ground on the other side, where the enemy barbed wire was. It seemed that he was condemned to inactivity.

He asked to be sent on patrol the following evening. The Captain laughed, saying that they would not get beyond the stream without drowning; it would be impossible even to swim in the reeds. They might perhaps find an easy passage, answered Wingult. As soon as it was quite dark they went down to the bed of reeds, but they found themselves getting stuck in the marshy ground everywhere and stood there water-logged. Wingult looked about him in displeasure. After some futile wading he beckoned to the others to remain where they were, and without a word disappeared downstream in the darkness up to his waist in the water. The dragoons waited patiently for a long time. Then suddenly there was a distinct movement over the flooded area; the water was beginning to flow off in slow circles. Shortly afterwards Wingult appeared again. Nobody knew what he had actually succeeded in doing, but it must have been a gigantic effort. He was black with slimy mud, blowing marshy water from his nose and mouth, his whole body quivering with the exertion he had made. At last he said that he had moved a stone out of position; but from the result he had achieved he must certainly have made a breach in the embankment.

Uneasy at the change in the water level, the enemy kept the marsh under heavy fire during the following day. As a new attack was being planned by the Germans, the troops were ordered to throw a narrow bridge across the stream, and in any case to have trestles, planks, and piers in readiness. During the following night the material required was brought to the edge of the reeds in a four-horse waggon and dumped there inconspicuously. The subaltern and Wingult had been detailed for this operation, and while the waggon was being unloaded two of the horses were killed by a shell. Wingult, who wanted to cross, said it would be better to build the bridge at once. The first piers were firm, and the planks laid across them carried as far as the edge of the marshy stream. To his dismay, however, Wingult observed that the next piers could not be secured to the bed of the stream; there was a patch of open water in the reeds which could not be sounded. Wingult looked about him, and had a wild inspiration for some kind of a floating bridge. He got off the planks and ordered two dragoons to help him. Lying almost prostrate, he pushed his head and neck under the chest of one of the dead horses. He put the front legs across his shoulders; supported behind by the two dragoons, the enormous carcass was carried on his back to the end of the bridge. Then Wingult dropped it over his neck into the marsh.

The little subaltern, who had stepped back with all the others, shuddered slightly, not so much at the sight itself as at the terrific idea which had emanated from such prodigious strength. The carcass, gently resting on the breaking reeds as on a bed, floated a tiny way downstream until it was held in position by the reeds.

Wingult proceeded to test whether the horse's body would bear the weight; and although it gave a little this floating pier carried two planks and the weight of a man, and when the man stepped off it rose again.

Wingult, however, was not satisfied. He repeated the operation, and bore the second dead horse on his back, slipping it over his neck into the reeds to lie beside the other. Then with poles and boards he pushed the whole conglomerate mass outwards and lay the two planks side by side across the intervening space, binding them securely to the planks which were resting on firm ground. The pier held and did not budge; the actual deep spot had been passed, and on the other side the piers got a grip in the soil.

Six times Wingult walked backwards and forwards across the bridge alone, as though to take formal possession. It was protected by the reeds, and even by day it would not have been detected.

Wingult took up a rifle and looked at the subaltern. At last he had got forward, he said, and he was not going to rear again. The subaltern, who was in command of the little squad that had been working on the bridge, understood what was in his mind, but he asked what his intentions were. 'I want to get across,' Wingult said, his mind full of vague deeds. 'Alone?' asked Salzach, not prepared to allow the others to go. 'Alone,' said Wingult.

The young officer looked at him with undisguised admiration. To him this seemed an almost impossible act of daring in which he could hardly hope to share. He was suddenly inspired to say, 'Only if I come too,' blushing in the pride of rivalry.

Wingult turned away and said nothing. He took two loaves from the car and, mindful of his young friend, took also a rug off one of the horses. In the morning before dawn and in the evening after dusk other members of the squad were to bring food up to the bridge. It would not be necessary for them to cross it, they would merely have to place the provisions at the end of the bridge. Wingult indicated the precise place. Then he made way for the young officer to cross the bridge in front of him with an air as though Salzach were a spectator who had no practical concern in the matter.

Leaving the reeds and the low-lying ground behind, they slowly mounted the gentle incline. Wingult settled himself into an old shell-hole behind a bush which had been uprooted by the explosion. When the night came he would be able to see from this spot what could be done. Little Salzach thrilled at the calm fearlessness with which his friend's great bodily strength fortified him; Wingult had no shudders of terror or disgust to fight down.

So far Wingult had gone his way unchecked, but the ration arrangements broke down. On the following morning, it is true, he found two well-filled bowls of soup that was still warm when he returned to the bridge after an uneventful night, but in the evening the spot where the food should have been was empty.

An hour before Salzach had been shot. The enemy may have noticed some incautious movement, or something else may have aroused his suspicions. In any case, the bush and the roots behind which they were lying were suddenly riddled with a burst of machine-gun fire, and one bullet lodged in the little subaltern's brain. In vain Wingult held his clumsy finger to the little round opening; it was the blood of a dead man that flowed from it.

When he returned to the bridge Wingult took his dead friend with him. How light he is, he thought; none of the hundreds of dead whom he had carried had been so light. He placed the body in the reeds, stretched out like a slim candle. They would come and fetch it, he thought. Then he looked for the rations, but the spot where they should have been was bare.

Wingult looked towards the German lines in dismay. All was quiet there; an occasional flare went up, to sink slowly and die out over the hollow. He supposed that there must have been some accidental delay, and hung the empty pans, out of which he and his officer had eaten, on the bridge post, returning with leisurely steps to his post. The next morning, too, he found nothing; the desolate pans hung there empty, and the subaltern's corpse was untouched. Again he looked over to the German trenches; they were not a quarter of an hour away. He was feeling hungry, the loaves were finished, but he never moved from the bridge. He wanted to know whether he had been forgotten and how far they would go. How could he know that the squadron had been hastily taken out of the line on the previous evening for other duties, and that different troops were occupying the trenches in which he supposed his companions to be; that they had received special instructions from those they were relieving to bring food for two men each day to the bridge in the hollow; and that the officer commanding the relieving troops had flatly forbidden this, as he was not going to risk a man for a couple of pots of food? It was incredible that there should be anyone over there, and if anyone was hungry he would come back all right. Of all this Wingult was certainly in complete ignorance; indeed, he returned to the spot which he had selected, and he kept pondering all day on the question why he was not brought any food. Time and again he went through his paybook to see to what duties the Emperor had committed him. But the book laid down no regulations, and if it had he would not have been able to read them. He tried to think whether they had neglected him before, but he remembered that one morning he had found his cooker filled full with fresh milk, which his companions had got at night by milking the peasants' cows; they must have gone a long way for it.

By the evening of the second day, when he went down to the bridge—he went late, lest he should arrive too early—his body was craving food and his mood was black. He found everything unchanged. He looked incredulously into the pots: they were as empty as on the day before. He turned them up and looked inside them again: they remained empty.

Then Wingult groaned—a deep, savage moan. Holding the pots in his enormous hands, he turned to the darkness, where were the German sentries, the advance troops, the armies, and away behind the land in which he had once been a child. He stretched himself and roared into the night like a monstrous wild beast. Then he dropped the pots.

After this he went to the dead body of the little subaltern at the end of the bridge. It was stiff with the rigor of death. Wingult raised it out of the reeds, and took it under his arm like a board; he turned about and crossed the swaying bridge of carcasses. Near the centre he stopped for a moment. Cautiously he placed the body in front of him on the planks, turned round clumsily, and looked back. As one about to make a fine farewell, he took a long pull at the bottle by his side. For a moment the sentries, who had been startled by his roar, saw the monstrous form of a man rising above the water; then the apparition vanished. But Wingult drove the stopper home into the bottle-neck with the flat of his hand, took up the dead body, and turned his back on the people whom he had served. He would seek other service, he thought sullenly. Slow and brooding he passed across with his dead friend under his arm; towards the enemy—into the darkness.

Walter Duranty

The Miracle

The General plucked at his moustache impatiently as he paced up and down the little brick-walled room. Two days ago he had moved from his comfortable quarters in the château behind the lines to the front *poste de commandement* in the cellars of a ruined farmhouse. It was mid-winter of 1915, and the sector for which he was responsible was thinly held against stronger German forces.

Twice had the General made urgent demands to the Army Headquarters for reinforcement. The position was critical, in this little salient where a break might affect the whole Arras line.

'Hasn't Captain Sarrail arrived yet?' he snapped at the orderly. 'You said Post 17 had reported his passage. Didn't you tell them he was to be admitted immediately?'

The blond young sergeant at the desk permitted himself an imperceptible shrug of ennui. The Old Man was getting fussy, he thought. Like a good soldier, he decided to show activity.

'I will make inquiries, *mon Général.*' He saluted and started toward the door.

At that moment it swung open. The General could not repress a movement of surprise. It is not usual to be saluted in the correct French military manner by a medieval saint. Before him stood a stony figure in a pilgrim's robe, the heavy folds rigid with grey plaster. The long beard was plaster too, and the face expressionless under its grey plaster cast. Only the eyes, bright and blue, were alive.

'What news?' cried the General.

'Nothing,' was the reply, flat and unhuman from behind the mask. The staring orderly shivered.

'Make your report, Captain,' the General said quietly.

'According to orders, one hour before dawn I mounted the façade of the ruined chapel at the cross roads on Sugar Loaf Hill, overlooking the enemy lines, in place of the statue of St Christopher, which we deposited in the crypt. As you know, sir, the chapel is only seventy-five metres from our advance posts, and my patrol was unmolested by the enemy, whose front-line trench is three hundred metres distant. As you had anticipated, it was not possible to arrange telephonic communication. The only figure left on the façade was right in the centre, away from any supports where the apparatus might have been concealed. The niche below it, where the crucifix stands, was too small for me. I remained in position until one hour after dark, but remarked no activity behind the German trenches, over which, as we thought, I had full view.'

He swayed slightly, and added: 'But it was very cold.'

'My dear fellow!' cried the General. 'How stupid of me! But you know how anxious I am. Quick, sergeant—fetch the brandy; there, under the table. And the coffee. Can you sit down, Sarrail?'

'No, sir,' said the other faintly, supporting himself against the desk. 'But with your permission we might take this off. It has to be done again for to-morrow in any case.'

With the help of the orderly the young officer wrenched off the pilgrim robe, and sat down. Two quick taps, and the beard fell away from his chin, which contrasted oddly with the plaster cast, still covering his nose and head.

He swallowed the steaming coffee and brandy in deep gulps.

'*B-rrr*,' he said. 'It is cold up there, *mon Général!*'

'Oh, those people in Paris!' raged his superior. 'Two weeks, now, they promise us observation balloons; but nothing comes. And our aeroplanes, they simply do not exist before these new German Fokkers.' Then, in a different tone: 'But it is not too much for you? You think you can stand it?'

The Captain rose to his feet. '*Mon Général*,' he said, and his voice now was stronger, 'when I volunteered for this work, I knew what it would mean. After to-day, I tell you it is not easy. But I know I can stand it for other days too.'

The General frowned. 'I don't know,' he said. 'It's so fantastic. After all, with your knowledge of German, don't you think you'd get more from this new microphone thing? At least you'd be under cover, instead of up there in full view.'

'As I told you, sir, that's the whole point. The statue is so familiar that they just don't see it. Except for a stray shot, there's no risk whatever. We proved that yesterday. And I can't hear anything through the microphone. Their line is too far off. This is the only way.'

'Well, you won't have long to wait. Let me see . . . It's Tuesday now; and at last the Army says reinforcements are coming to reach us on Friday afternoon. So if they wait until then, we can hold them. But now'—he threw his hands out hopelessly—'if they put their whole weight on one point, and we are not prepared to meet them there—meet them *there*, I tell you—they'll break us. We cannot stop them. And if we go, the whole line cracks. It is disaster.'

'I know, sir. That is why I must go through with this.'

'But how can you stay up there all the time, without moving? It's fifteen feet from the ground, isn't it?'

'We drove hooks in the wall behind me,' said the Captain, 'and hitched them to this belt under my arms. I'd never have been able to stand without it, as the ledge is less than a foot wide.'

The General walked over to the map on the wall. 'The Sugar Loaf is a hundred and eighty feet above the trench level. Fifteen more—call it two hundred. Yes, you ought to be able to see from there.'

'I did, *mon Général*.'

'I suppose they must come on our right, along the main road. If the marsh on the left is frozen, their infantry might pass; but machine-guns and cannon, no. It is frozen, I suppose?'

'Yes, sir. But not enough yet for guns. Sergeant Pataud was out with a small patrol just after dark. He said the surface was quite firm in most places, but one of his men fell through into a ditch where the water was deeper. It certainly wouldn't bear heavy weights.'

The General sighed with relief. 'Yes,' he said, 'the attack will surely be along the road. I must plan to meet them there. If only I knew for certain!' . . .

It was cold on the chapel wall overlooking the desolate valley, with its ruined buildings, tangled wire, and black shell-craters in the frost-grey fields. As it grew light, Sarrail could see the German lines, with the curls of yellow smoke where breakfast was cooking. The marsh on his left was still hidden by a fog-bank, gradually being dispersed by the morning wind that swept across the plains of Flanders.

It was strangely quiet and empty, this landscape which concealed thousands of men preparing for battle. As the morning hours dragged by, the front grew more lively. Shells began to burst along the enemy wire, and beyond them he noted the great mushrooms of black smoke with their core of flame which meant the heavier French guns were raking communication lines haphazard.

The German guns made little response. No good sign, he thought. They must be nearly ready to attack, and anxious to keep their batteries hidden.

About noon he heard a thrumming high overhead, as four German battle-planes crossed the line. Of French airmen no sign. It was hard to stand motionless in the cold, without getting sleepy and stupefied. Luckily the belt across his chest held him firm, and the plaster from feet to waist kept his knees from sagging. The time moved slowly, so slowly, with little to mark its passing. A sudden burst of three French shells, on the slope of the hill below, roused him. This was their signal that it was two o'clock—only three more hours till dark, or four at the most. And still he had nothing to report.

He strained his eyes eastward, but the white road behind the German trenches stretching up to the wood on the hill was empty. Once he distinguished four figures at intervals of fifty yards, stepping warily amidst the French shell-bursts. Did this mean anything? A last-minute staff inspection? Of course they would have left their car in the wood. But that gave him small help. It was not *when* the attack came, but *where*, that mattered most.

Perhaps the General was right, and this plan of his was fool-hardy and worthless. Had the General said that? Something of the sort, anyway. A kind old man, though, to think of the bottle and the tube.

The shivering saint took a suck at the tube concealed by his plaster beard. The mixture of coffee, soup, and cognac sent a thrill of warmth through his body, and for a second he chuckled over a vision of the General as a benevolent papa, feeding a bottle to a fully equipped *poilu* in a man-sized cradle.

The minutes dragged. Would twilight never come? He was startled by a rattle of machine-gun fire from the German trenches on his left. He saw a handful of dark figures from the nearest French post, dodging forward among the rushes on the frozen marsh.

'*Mon Dieu*, the Old Man must be nervous, to send them out in broad daylight. Perhaps he wants to test the ice,' thought the watcher.

A moment later shells were bursting along the German tren-ches, and their machine-guns slackened. To Sarrail's surprise, a line of grey-clad men ran out in open order from the enemy trench. The fire grew hotter, and he caught the flash and crack of grenades in the rushes.

He took a deep suck at the tube. Why, this was a regular fight! But what did it mean? Was the marsh the place, not the road? If not, why should they counter-attack a mere scouting patrol? There must be something behind it. *Nom de Dieu!* Supposing they were trying trench-mortars or cannon on the marsh the night before, and wanting to hide their tracks? Yes, that might be it. Each day of this frost hardened the marsh.

The volume of fire redoubled. Every gun for miles was roaring now, and the air was full of the scream of passing shells. Another grey wave rose from the German wire, in column this time, rushing along the hillside to cut off the French patrol. Many fell, but the others ran on and spread fanwise among the rushes. Sarrail could see the sharp red spit of revolvers, and once or twice the flicker of steel. The French were trapped and outnumbered. Not a chance of—

A heavy fist hit him suddenly on the right side of his body. Despite himself, his head jerked sideways—there was no one there. Amazed, he looked down. A hand's-breadth of plaster had been split off halfway between his thigh and shoulder, and a red stain was spreading slowly over the white wool beneath. And there was something warm and salty in his mouth.

Instinctively he spat. A blob of red appeared between his feet. Then he knew, although he felt no pain.

He took a deep breath, and a knife stabbed through his chest up into his throat and brain. In that agony he choked and fainted. . . .

It was still daylight when his eyes opened. The pain was duller now, but constant, a deep ache all over his right side. He took small, cautious breaths. The taste of blood kept rising to his mouth, but he could keep his windpipe clear. Above all, not to cough or choke—and to wait for dusk.

He tried sucking the rubber tube, slowly, not more than a spoonful at a time. He was able to swallow. The liquid gave him strength, and his brain cleared. A bullet in the lungs—pretty bad. But there were worse wounds. If they carried him carefully, as he and young Mercier had carried Rousseau—at that, Rousseau had choked once. Yet Rousseau had recovered, was all right again. Flying now, somewhere. They took only healthy men to fly. Damn them, why were there no planes here? Were they all afraid of the Germans?

Another sip from the tube. Ah, that was better . . . He wasn't done yet; he'd show them.

There was no sign of movement now, in the marsh. Had any of the patrol got back? Probably not. Well, he had something to tell. The attack would be there. They'd never have used such force on a mere patrol unless—Oh, God, this pain! He hardly dared to breathe. Why couldn't the darkness come?

Great heavens, what was that? Despite his pain, he gave a feeble chuckle. It was so comic and unexpected. A hundred yards below, on the white edge of the marsh, a small figure was running in crazy zigzags, like a wounded rabbit. It ran forward, then straight back; then right, then left.

Forgetting his wound, he watched intently. The man, if it was a man, had fallen and was beating the ground with his feet and hands. Sarrail sucked again at the tube. Was he delirious, or was the dusk playing tricks with his eyes? No, it was true; it was a man—in German uniform—running straight towards him, up the hill.

A sudden fear—could they have guessed, somehow? But no. He could see the blown red face and staring eyes.

The advancing figure stopped, and looked straight up at him. Perhaps, after all, he did guess . . . No. The man ran a few steps more, and flung himself upon his knees before the crucifix, underneath Sarrail.

At first Sarrail could catch no meaning in the stream of words poured forth in a crazy falsetto babble. Then, gradually, he began to understand. Sin and terror were the burden of the pitiful tale. God had punished the suppliant . . . That night at mess, when they questioned God's mercy, he had not protested. He had sinned, and been punished.

The voice rose to a scream as it told of long nights when prayer was powerless to drive out fear, and days when men with torn bodies died blaspheming in filth and blood. He could bear no more. That Frenchman to-day on the marsh—his face as Schmidt stamped on his body to wrench the bayonet out. And to-morrow—oh, God, to-morrow! Killing again, smashing them under the wheels. Oh, God! Oh, Christ, have pity!

Sarrail's brain was burning. The marsh—the wheels—the wheels across the marsh! He must hold out until they came.

Surely it was darker. The German line was hidden, and the marsh a whitish blur. In an hour they must be coming. But this German—what would he do? Would he give the alarm? Was he—

The kneeling man began to speak again, less wildly now. Was it all a lie, his faith? No God in heaven, no hope, no mercy? Was God a lie? How could he tell or know?

He was silent for a time, then held up his hands in prayer. Speaking slowly, like a child, he began: 'Our Father, which art in

Heaven, I pray Thee, help me now. I have sinned in Thy sight, and been punished. It is Thy will. Only give me a sign that Thou art God—a sign to hold my faith.'

He bowed until his forehead was touching the ground at the foot of the crucifix. Sarrail tried to lean forward to watch him, and his wound gave a sudden throb.

From below came a whisper of amazement. 'It is blood—blood!' A space of silence, then a loud, ecstatic cry: 'Thy blood upon my head! I thank Thee for this sign!'

He sprang to his feet, crossed himself, and said firmly: 'It is enough.' Then he turned and walked with resolute steps into the darkness towards the German lines.

Sarrail was weaker now, scarcely conscious. Had he dreamed all this? Would his comrades never come, and could he live to give them his message?

Colonel von Stron stood at the top of the stairs leading to his dug-out, and sniffed the frosty air. 'Good,' he said. 'Very good!'

He went down the stairs and tapped the barometer hanging on the wall. 'Good,' he repeated. 'Set fair. The frost will hold.'

He took a sheaf of papers from the table and began to check them off against the lines of little flags pinned into a map on the wall. Suddenly the telephone rang.

'Hello! . . . Yes? . . . Is that the Army? . . . I was expect—What? Speak up, man! . . . You know I'm busy . . . What? Father Holze? . . . Well, tell him I can't. I'm too busy . . . What? . . . Then stop him . . . Then you should have done.' And he slammed the receiver back.

Frowning, the Colonel called to his aide. 'Lieutenant Hilger, I've just had a message from the line that Father Holze is on his way to see me. You will meet him and explain that I'm too busy. Doesn't he know that we attack at dawn to-morrow? And I'm expecting a call from Headquarters. But—put it nicely. Ach, these Bavarians! Do you think one of our Prussian chaplains would bother his C.O. at a time like this?'

His subordinate smiled. 'Certainly, sir, I'll attend to it.' He saluted and was gone.

Von Stron went back to his work. He took a piece of red chalk and drew a line across the map, scribbled at the end '6 *p.m.*,' and moved up a row of flags.

'If that's right,' he muttered, 'and it must be, we'll be at Arras in forty-eight hours. Now I'm ready for Headquarters.'

He sat down. Everything was ready. At dawn the smashing

blow—the French taken by surprise and breaking . . . Then, *General* von Stron! The youngest General in the Army!

Voices on the staircase disturbed him. The door flew open, and a small, red-faced man burst in.

The Colonel rose to his feet. 'Father Holze,' he said stiffly, 'I am surprised—'

The priest put out his hand. 'I know how busy you are, Colonel, But this is different. You must hear me.'

Von Stron stared down at him. 'You understand, sir, I gave orders I was not to be interrupted. Urgent affairs—'

The priest ignored the rebuff. 'The affairs of God,' he said, 'come first. I am here with Lieutenant Grosner. You must see him.'

The Colonel frowned. 'Grosner? Grosner! You may not know, Father Holze, that Lieutenant Grosner deserted his men in action in a most—'

Again he was checked. 'You shall judge for yourself,' said the priest, 'but you must see him. I insist.'

For a moment Von Stron's eyes were dark with anger. Then he said curtly. 'Very well. Bring him in.'

Expressionless, the Colonel eyed the muddy, dishevelled young officer. There was a smear of blood across his forehead. He did not salute.

The Colonel waited.

Grosner met his eyes. 'I have come back,' he said.

'Yes,' said Von Stron, watching him.

'I have seen a miracle.'

'Go on.'

'They said there was no God, because He could not allow this War. There *is* a God. I saw the miracle.'

'Go on,' said the Colonel, watching his rapt eyes.

'I prayed at the chapel on the hill, because I had left my men, and lost God, and it was dark. I asked for a sign, and the blood fell on my head. Now I must tell my comrades.'

Von Stron watched him.

'I shall show them His blood here,' said Grosner, touching the stain across his forehead.

'What's that?' asked the Colonel sharply.

'I was praying to the crucifix, beneath the big saint on the wall, because I had lost my faith. I begged God for a sign, to save me. And His blood fell upon my head. So I came back to tell them. That is all.'

'That is all?' repeated the Colonel.

'That is all.'

The clock ticked on through an interminable silence.

Suddenly Von Stron's fist crashed on the desk. 'It's true! Of course it's true! Now I see it,' he shouted, and snatched the telephone.

'Give me the advance post—urgent!... Hello! Is that Forstner? ... Yes, Von Stron speaking. Take a strong patrol immediately, without losing a moment, to the chapel on the hill. Examine the wall and the crucifix and the saint's statue. Look for blood signs on the ground. See if they're fresh ... Just do as I tell you at once. And send back a runner to report.'

He turned to the bewildered priest. 'Your miracle is French,' he said, 'and his sign is French too. Take him away. I leave him in your charge.'

He made a discouraged gesture, and added, as if thinking aloud: 'I'm afraid it's that. Unless they get him, we're done. It's too late now to change the plan.'

In the darkness above the crucifix the lonely figure hung unmoving, fastened to the wall.

A clink of metal against stone. Dark, shuffling forms, and a soft French voice, '*Mon Capitaine,* we have come.'

No reply. Silence. And on the frosty ground a broad stain.

They set the ladder against the wall and lowered the heavy figure to the ground.

A whisper: 'Is he dead?'

'I don't know. Give me the cognac.'

Sarrail's eyes opened. He gasped.

'Listen,' he breathed.

The man put his ear close to the whitened lips.

'You hear me, yes? ... Tell General—attack—attack—'

'Yes, *mon Capitaine,* I hear you.'

'Attack—across marsh—to-morrow—certain—'

The listener repeated: 'Tell—General—attack—across—marsh—to-morrow—certain.'

Sarrail's eyes closed; and opened again. They were carrying him carefully as he and Mercier had carried Rousseau; and soon a surgeon had him in care.

Axel Eggebrecht

Death of a Cat

Houthoulst Forest was the heart of that ravaged earth. There all horrors met and flowed together; trickled ceaselessly from a livid sky, flowed through broken dykes and oozed untiringly from an earth which absorbed what it discharged with a depraved thirst.

The horror was wetness. Dryness would have been Paradise, an unimaginable alleviation to demoralized nerves. But nothing was dry. The damp bread went mouldy overnight; the plum and apple jam swelled and burst its tins; worst of all was the greasy leather, which the damp once more resolved into unsavoury strips of dead beasts, exhaling the fetid, sweetish odour of mildewed corpses.

This sodden corner of the earth was also, by the illogical dictates of war, a strategic point on the fighting front. Limbs were blown off and shattered for it, as they were being shattered all over Europe—in Lorraine, in Macedonia, in the Ukraine. But there they were at least embedded in the sheltering earth—that earth which they had never touched in their jerry-built houses, their concrete factories, and their asphalt streets. When they were cast, by sheer physical revolt, upon her whom poets still call mother, she, at least, would not reject them.

But even this comfort was denied us. Flanders was not earth; Flanders was paste. Here even the almighty mother was dissolved, disintegrated, and enfeebled, so that she could support us no longer.

If you threw yourself down, even in those places designated on the maps as 'firm ground', you would sense, not that sudden invigorating contact with solid earth, but the sucking embrace of mud cushions with the slimy water flowing endlessly away.

Nevertheless, we did lie down to sleep. The ceaseless trickle of water did not waken us, although our legs swelled and our flesh grew morbid and discoloured. We did not die, we did not even fall sick; only we ceased to talk to each other, passing by with nothing but a grunt. It was as though the spoken word were an unbearable superfluity in an existence so futile and so precarious.

Such was our condition when there came to us the incredible

hope of sleeping once more in the dry. One night, as we went forward in single file to relieve a section in an advanced gun outpost, we suddenly collapsed on top of each other in a shock of joy. Our happiness made us once more articulate; we talked, we uttered whole sentences. In front of us was a hole, a dry hole, ten yards long, roofed over. The walls, it was true, dripped with damp, but on the ground yellow straw was strewn thickly for a couch. It was quite evident that we were to sleep there.

The hole proved to be the remains of a tunnelling through a dyke. It was knee-deep in water, but our predecessors had built wooden trestles on which we threw ourselves immediately. The surface of that loathsome element from which we had at last escaped lay three spans below.

All fourteen of us fell asleep and dreamed—fourteen, warm, bright dreams of throats that could once more feel thirst, of skins that could once more feel dust and heat, of burning, golden sands with green-blue oases. Hands that had become flaccid and nerveless found sensual pleasure in stroking the fabric of our uniforms, now almost dry.

My head was burning; I was panting along in the dust of an unending road in a welter of dry, pitiless heat. Each moment I was becoming browner, drier, shrivelling in that supernatural sun. The dryness had ceased to be grateful, and then . . . just at the right moment, a finger touched me—a cool, slender finger, like a little fragment of a snake. It was a dark enchantress who had put her finger into her mouth and then trailed its sinister coolness across my throat. The sun's heat had waned, the dust was thickening and swelling into a myriad of sluggish raindrops, and still that cold, snake-like finger stroked my throat and my lips and my face . . .

Then I started up. Something heavy ran down my legs and fell with a loud plop off the wooden platform. The pointed dark thing that was so strange to me had slid out of my dreams into the water. Someone in the corner shouted: 'Hell! Rats!'

And so that night became transmuted into the night of our deepest despair. We had found refuge from the wet, we had escaped to a world where we could once more dream of dryness, but out of that loathsome liquid beneath our sleeping bodies the obscene creatures emerged, rested their weight impudently upon our limbs, and drew their slimy tails across our mouths. They upset the coffee-pot and nibbled at the bread. We put it into a bag and hung it from the roof, that beloved roof which kept the streaming sky from us. But scarcely had we fallen asleep again when once more the running and the scratching began; by twos and threes they leapt up at the desirable bundle, falling with horrid little plops into the water below.

A couple of us decided to remain awake, keeping off sleep by retailing horrid accounts of rats that had eaten off children's hands and the eyes out of living calves, tales of plague and cholera. Suddenly the speaker ceased. He seemed to see, at the end of the wooden bench, a sharp, malignant face, listening with an approving grin while its beady eyes winked an unqualified concurrence.

There was a moment's silence. Then he snatched his revolver and fired it two or three times. We all jumped up in panic, crowding out of the hole, and relieving ourselves with a burst of wild, aimless shooting. Then we quietened down and returned, to find the trestles strewn with patches of wet lime, while our bread dropped lamentably through the holes of the shot-ridden sack. Two dirty-white little taut bellies were floating about in the water; we flung them outside.

Once more I fell asleep, then, a quarter of an hour later, that disgusting familiar pressure once more intruded upon my dreaming consciousness—damp little feet and a pointed, waving tail. I tried not to awaken, although, as a matter of fact, I was awake already. I kept my eyes shut and tried to hold my breath, but in the end my nerves forced me to get up. I groped my way out, threw a coat over me, and squatted down for the rest of the night out there in the rain.

Some nights later, Moogk, who was splashing up and down on sentry duty, noticed something peculiar moving about in the fitful light cast by distant flares. With the usual curiosity of the soldier in the front line he ran after it, saw it run off in a zigzag course and disappear in the ruins of what was once the village, but was now a shapeless heap of bricks. For a moment two green eyes had glared at him, and he suddenly turned round and rushed back to us as fast as the clay and mud would let him. I happened to be the first man he met, and he grabbed me excitedly by the arm, his hoarse voice eager with his great news. *There was a cat in the village.*

Three minutes later we were all scrambling about among the bricks looking for it.

On such a night as this the drenched Flemish carriers must have crowded in at the inn door, invoking the Blessed Virgin as they poured the rough spirit down their chilled throats. With their great heavy boots they probably kicked the little cat out of the way as she crowded in among them, hating the cold and the wet as much as they. Perhaps it would rush past them into the warm inn-parlour, refusing to be scared by any display of violence. They had gone now, but it remained, roaming among the bricks and the debris and the shell-holes as though they were the currant bushes in the garden. It had refused to be driven away by shells and bullets, but now that fourteen human wraiths were flittering once more about the remains of that human habitation, trying to coax it with friendly calls as though all were well again, the animal huddled in the deepest and most inaccessible cleft of its labyrinth. We called it and searched for it in vain; it mewed piteously, but it would not come. At last we withdrew and threw ourselves back on our wooden couch, beneath which lurked the filthy creatures of the flood.

But that gave us something to talk about. If the cat had been there in the flesh we might have felt a little foolish in confessing that her wholesome fur coat crystallized for us all our longing for warmth and dryness in that place of loathsome damp; that she seemed like a guardian appointed to drive off the obscene devils of that unnatural underworld. But we felt that we could speculate and indulge our fancies freely while we were still uncertain whether she were anything but a creature of Moogk's imagination.

The following night she was seen by two others. In fact, we must have been surrounded by whole battalions of cats, so many were the conflicting reports about large cats, small cats, coal-black cats, snow-white cats, spotted cats, and every other strange and commonplace variety of the animal. Our affection deepened to positive worship; we expressed it by cutting off bits of our rare and exiguous meat ration as votive offerings to the goddess, the offerings being placed in prominent places far removed from our profane dwelling. At first they were spurned, for did we not bear the brand of Cain, and how could our sacrifice prove acceptable? But in the end the goddess relented, and the dedicated morsels began to vanish. Before dawn she would sometimes even prowl around our hole, while we waited inside breathlessly. But if one of us moved towards her she would disappear in a couple of bounds, contemptuous of our dismay.

So things went on for a few days. The rats wandered about, quite indifferent to the fact that we were darkly planning their extermination. Then we called a council, prompted by Heaven knows what atavistic survival from a primitive past, to discuss whether we might compel the goddess to come to us. Opinion was divided; but when Moogk, the first harbinger of salvation, declared himself in agreement, the holy chase was approved.

In the early morning we circled round the ruins of the inn, armed with all sorts of instruments for noise-making. One of the men actually took a flare, to which, however, he meant to have recourse only in extreme emergency.

We were standing, in the growing daylight, gazing upon the dirty pile of bricks in a state of excitement which we had believed to be long since forgotten. We were waiting for Moogk's shout, and he was standing, like a true militant prophet, with arm upraised in the damp stillness.

We waited tensely for him to lower it, but instead he himself crumpled up on the ground, and at that very moment, at seven thirty-six of that cold, wet morning, the most terrible bombardment of the winter campaign began. Like a striking clock, timed to the second, the British offensive was set in motion, and the pile of bricks that housed our goddess was levelled to the ground.

We ran through a curtain of burning splinters that hummed round our heads. I stumbled and fell among the bricks, and as I lay there I noticed that all the fourteen men were not running back to the hole. Some had been wounded and fallen; I, crawling painfully along, was the last to get in. As I pulled the door to, a ridiculous gesture to heighten the false security of being under cover, a soft thing slipped through my hands and cowered with wild eyes in the corner, where it glanced from one to another.

There, between the six of us who had come through safely, lay the cat, a draggled bundle of pure terror—a terror so acute that it became infectious.

None of us thought of approaching her. Outside the world was collapsing; we sat huddled together without thought. Some time later the door was flung open by men hurrying past. They signed to us to follow, and so we joined in the retreat that had been ordered. At the last moment I wanted to take the cat in my arms, but at the first movement of my outstretched hand she retreated so wildly that she slipped off the wooden platform. I can still see the stark horror in her eyes as she fell, but there was no time to do anything. Torn by remorse, I had to rush out, close the door, and run for my life.

Eight or ten hours later the attack was checked. It was night before we returned, and as we approached the hole, dead tired as we were, I was conscious of an extraordinary sense of expectation. I ran on in front of the others, pulled open the door, and flashed a light. A fat rat grinned at my torch, turned slowly round, and dropped off into the water.

We flashed our torches round all the corners, but in vain, and, as though by agreement, all our lights were extinguished suddenly together. We did not say anything about the vanished one, but lay down in sulky silence on the boards. I lay awake for a long time before the rhythm of approaching sleep began to beat upon my senses—I was numbed as if by an anaesthetic—and then, just at the moment when I was sinking into oblivion, turning unconsciously on my other side as I have always done since childhood, I sensed a pressure on my shoulder. I leapt up, wide awake.

I could not keep back the shriek of terror that rose so suddenly, almost before I could draw my breath. All the torches flashed out in panic. My hand grasped a little round white skull.

It was smooth and polished clean, scratched with a thousand little marks like a scalpel. I could still feel the pressure under my shoulder, and now that the lights showed up every corner of the place I could see little white bones strewn all over the straw.

Like a man caught in some monstrous act of betrayal, I held the little white skull in my hands. They trembled as though I should never again be able to control them. One of the men said slowly:

'And she didn't want to fight at all.'

We looked at one another, and the unchecked tears were streaming down our cheeks.

Alphonse Daudet

The Boy Spy

He was called Stenne: Little Stenne. He was a boy of Paris, sickly looking and pallid, who could have been ten years old—or perhaps even fifteen. With midges like that you can never tell. His mother was dead; his father, an ex-marine, was caretaker of a garden square in the Temple quarter. The children, the nursemaids, the old ladies in deck-chairs, the poor mothers—all the people who took refuge from the traffic among those flower-bordered walks—they all knew old Papa Stenne, and adored him.

They knew that beneath the shaggy moustache there lurked a generous, almost maternal, smile—and that to provoke that smile they had only to ask the dear old fellow: 'How's your little son?' The old man was so very fond of that boy of his! He was never so happy as in the evenings, when the boy came for him after school, and the pair of them strolled along the paths, halting at every seat and bench to have a word with the regulars.

But when the Prussians besieged Paris, everything changed utterly. Papa Stenne's square was closed and taken as an oil-store. The poor old fellow spent all his time on guard, not even able to smoke—and only getting a glimpse of his boy late at night. As for the Prussians, the old man's moustache used positively to bristle when he talked of *them*. But Little Stenne, on the other hand, didn't find all that much to grumble about in the changed conditions.

A siege! It was a great lark for the kids! No more school! No more homework! One long holiday, and the streets like a fairground.

The boy was out of doors playing the whole day. He used to accompany the local battalions whenever they marched off to the ramparts—preferably any battalion that had a good band, a subject on which Little Stenne was an expert. He could tell you emphatically that the band of the 98th wasn't much good, but that the 55th had a pretty good one. At other times, he would cast an eye at the reserves doing their drill, and there were always the queues to join.

With a shopping-basket on his arm, he would tag on to those long queues outside the butcher's or the baker's and there, scuffling his feet in the gutter, he would meet people and earnestly discuss the situation—for being the son of Papa Stenne his opinion was always sought. Best of all were the games of *galoche*—a game in which you had to bowl over a cork with money on it and which the Breton reservists had made popular during the siege.

Whenever Little Stenne wasn't on the ramparts or queueing at the baker's, you could be sure of finding him at some *galoche* tournament in Water-Tower Square. He didn't take part—that would have needed too much money. He just looked on, and he particularly admired one of the players, a big lad in a blue coat who invariably gambled with five-franc pieces and nothing else. When that boy ran you could hear the money jingling in his coat-pockets.

One day, as Little Stenne retrieved a coin that had rolled near the boy, the big fellow muttered to him: 'That makes you stare, eh? If you like, I'll show you where to find some more.'

At the end of the game he strolled away with Little Stenne and asked him if he'd like to go with him and sell newspapers to the Prussians, who would pay anyone thirty francs for the trouble. To begin with, Little Stenne refused indignantly—and he was so upset by the offer that he kept away from the game for several days. Terrible days they were—he couldn't eat or sleep for thinking about it all.

At night in bed he could see nothing but heaps of corks and glittering five-franc pieces. He couldn't resist the temptation. On the fourth day he went back to Water-Tower Square, spoke to the big lad again, and this time was easily persuaded.

One snowy morning the two of them started out with sacks over their shoulders and newspapers hidden in their clothes. Dawn had scarcely broken when they arrived at a place called the Pâte de Flandres on the outskirts of the city. The big boy took Little Stenne by the hand and approached the kindly looking, red-nosed French sentry.

'Here, mister,' he said in a whining tone, 'can we go on? Mother's ill and our old man's dead. My kid brother and I want to see if we can find some spuds in the fields out there.'

He started blubbering—and Little Stenne drooped his head in shame. The sentry eyed them for a moment, then glanced down the deserted, snow-covered road.

'All right, off with you,' he said, dismissing them—and straightaway they were on the road to Aubervilliers. The older boy nearly laughed himself silly.

Bewildered, as if in a dream, Little Stenne caught sight of factories that had been taken over as barracks, ramshackle barricades, towering chimneys that pierced the mist and groped into the sky. Here and there were more sentries, officers surveying the distance through telescopes, little tents wet from melted snow near half-hearted fires.

The big lad knew all the roads and short-cuts, but even so it wasn't his fault that they ran into a platoon of light infantry crouching in a trench alongside the Soissons railway. Although he told his story all over again the soldiers wouldn't let them pass. The big lad put up a show of crying again, and a sergeant, grizzled and white-haired, rather like old Papa Stenne, emerged from the level-crossing keeper's house to see what was going on.

'All right, kids,' he said, when he had listened to their story, 'stop all that noise. You can go and get your potatoes. But come in and warm yourselves first—that little fellow looks frozen!'

But it wasn't with cold that Little Stenne was shivering, it was with shame and fear. In the guardhouse, more soldiers were squatting round a miserable fire, trying to thaw out their bone-hard biscuits on the point of their bayonets. They moved over to make room for the boys, and gave them a mouthful of coffee. While they were drinking, an officer stuck his head in the door and beckoned to the Sergeant with whom he had a rapid, whispered conversation.

'Well, lads!' the Sergeant cried, rubbing his hands. 'We're going to have some fun tonight. They've got hold of the Prussian password and, if you ask me, we're going to recapture blessed old Bourget again, where we've had so many scraps in the past.'

The place echoed with cheers and exultant laughter. The soldiers began to polish their bayonets, singing and dancing as they did so, and in the midst of the tumult the boys took themselves off.

Beyond the trench lay nothing but the empty plain and in the distance a long white wall pierced with loop-holes. Pretending to be gathering potatoes, they made their way towards this wall. All the time Little Stenne kept urging the big lad to go back, but he only shrugged his shoulders and pressed on. All at once they heard the rattle of a rifle being cocked.

'Down!' said the big lad, flinging himself to the ground.

Lying there, he whistled. An answering whistle came across the snow. They crawled forward on hands and knees. In front of the wall, at ground level, a pair of yellow moustaches under a crumpled cap appeared. The big lad jumped down into the trench alongside the Prussian.

'This kid's my brother,' he said, jerking a thumb at Little Stenne.

Little Stenne was so small that the Prussian laughed at him—and had to take him in his arms to help him in.

On the other side of the breastwork there were strong earth ramparts reinforced with tree-trunks and in between them, fox-holes, occupied by more yellow-moustached German soldiers in their crumpled caps.

In one corner of the fortification was a gardener's lodge, also supported with tree-trunks. On the ground floor more soldiers were playing cards or making soup on a blazing fire. The boiled cabbage and lard smelt good—very different from the poverty-stricken cooking-fire of the French infantrymen. Upstairs the officers could be heard strumming at a piano amid the popping of champagne corks.

When the two boys from Paris entered the room they were greeted with shouts of glee. They delivered their newspapers and were given drinks and encouraged to talk. All the officers looked haughty and formidable, but the big lad kept them amused with his cheeky ways and gutter slang. They roared with laughter, imitated his words, and revelled in the tittle-tattle he had brought from Paris.

Little Stenne would have liked to join in the talk, to show them he wasn't stupid either, but something held him back. Before him sat a Prussian who seemed more serious than the rest of them, and though he was pretending to read, his eyes never left Little Stenne. There was a kind of reproachful tenderness in those eyes, as if the man had a boy of his own at home and was thinking to himself: 'I'd rather be dead than see a son of mine acting like this.'

From that moment, Little Stenne felt as if a hand was pressing against his heart and prevented it from beating.

In order to get away from this pain, he gulped down his drink. Before long everything seemed to be whirling round him. He heard vaguely, to the accompaniment of laughter, his comrade mocking the French National Guard; giving an imitation of a call to arms in the Marais quarter of Paris; a night alarum on the ramparts. Eventually the big lad dropped his voice and the officers bent towards him with faces suddenly stern. The wretched youth was in the act of warning them of the infantrymen's intended attack.

At this Little Stenne leapt to his feet, angry and clear-headed: 'Not that, you great fool!' he cried. 'I won't let you . . .'

But the other simply guffawed and continued his story. Before he had completed it, all the officers were standing up. One of them ushered the boys to the door.

'Off with you, out of the camp!' he ordered them, and the officers began to talk rapidly among themselves in German. The big lad strode out, proud of himself and clinking his money. Little Stenne followed him, shamefaced, and as he passed the Prussian officer whose gaze had distressed him, he heard him saying mournfully: 'Not good, that . . . not good,' and the tears came into young Stenne's eyes.

Out on the plain the boys started to run and quickly made their way back. Their sacks were full of potatoes the Prussians had given them and they got past the infantrymen's trench without difficulty. The men were getting ready for the attack that night. Troops were coming up under cover and massing near the railway. The old Sergeant was there, busy giving orders with a keen air of anticipation. He recognized the boys as they passed and gave them a friendly grin.

That grin hurt Little Stenne deeply. For a moment he was minded to cry out in warning: 'Don't carry out the attack . . . we've given you away.' But the big lad had said to him: 'If you say anything now they'd shoot us,' and fear prevented him from acting.

At Corneneuve they entered a deserted house and divided the money. It must be admitted that once he could hear those fine five-franc pieces jingling in his pockets, Little Stenne no longer felt so bad.

But later, when he was on his own, misery swept over him. When, inside the city gates, the lad had left him, then his pockets seemed to grow terribly heavy . . . and that hand which gripped his heart was tighter than ever. Paris was no longer the same city in his eyes. The passers-by seemed to look at him harshly as if they knew where he'd been. Spy—spy—spy! He could hear the word everywhere about him, in the sound of passing wheels, in the beating of drums being played along the canal. At last he reached home. Relieved to find that his father had not yet come back, he went swiftly upstairs to their room and hid under his pillow the money that weighed so ponderously on his conscience.

Papa Stenne had never been so warm-hearted and jolly as he was that evening. News had arrived from the provinces that things had taken a turn for the better. While he ate, the old marine glanced at his musket hanging on the wall, and remarked with a laugh: 'Well, my boy, you'd go for those Prussians right enough if you were older, eh?'

Towards eight o'clock there was the sound of cannon-fire.

'Hello? That's Aubervilliers. There's fighting at Bourget,' said the old fellow, for he knew all the forts.

Little Stenne grew pale and, pretending he was very tired, took himself off to bed. But he couldn't sleep. The guns thundered on and on. He saw in his mind's eye the French infantrymen setting out under cover of darkness to surprise the Prussians—and themselves falling into an ambush. He remembered the old Sergeant who had grinned at him . . . and he could see him spreadeagled on the snow and many others with him . . . and the price of their blood was hidden there, under his very pillow. It was he, the son of Papa Stenne, ex-marine, who had betrayed them.

He was choked by tears. He heard his father moving about in the next room, opening a window. Down below in the square a call to arms rang out. A battalion of reservists was mustering urgently. Obviously a real battle was going on. The miserable boy could not contain his sobbing.

'What's it all about, then?' Papa Stenne demanded, entering the bedroom.

Little Stenne could bear it no longer. He leapt out of bed and flung himself at his father's feet. As he did so some of the money rolled to the floor.

'Hello? What's this? Have you been thieving?' the old man asked sharply, beginning to tremble.

Then, breathlessly, Little Stenne recounted how he had visited the Prussians, and what had happened there. As he uttered the words he felt his heart grow lighter. His confession made things easier to bear.

With a fearful expression Papa Stenne listened to the confession. At the end of it he bowed his head in his hands and wept silently.

'Father . . . father . . .' began the boy. But the old man repulsed him without a word and slowly gathered up the coins.

'Is this all?' was his only question.

Little Stenne nodded. The old man reached down his gun and his bandolier and put the money in his pocket. 'Ah, well,' he said,

'I am going to return it to them.'

Without speaking another word, without even a backward glance, he went down to the street to join the reservists who were setting off that night. He was never seen again.

Ambrose Bierce

The Affair at Coulter's Notch

'Do you think, Colonel, that your brave Coulter would like to put one of his guns in here?' the general asked.

He was apparently not altogether serious; it certainly did not seem a place where any artillerist, however brave, would like to put a gun. The colonel thought that possibly his division commander meant good-humouredly to intimate that in a recent conversation between them Captain Coulter's courage had been too highly extolled.

'General,' he replied warmly, Coulter would like to put a gun anywhere within reach of those people,' with a motion of his hand in the direction of the enemy.

'It is the only place,' said the general. He was serious, then.

The place was a depression, a 'notch,' in the sharp crest of a hill. It was a pass, and through it ran a turnpike, which reaching this highest point in its course by a sinuous ascent through a thin forest made a similar, though less steep, descent toward the enemy. For a mile to the left and a mile to the right, the ridge, though occupied by Federal infantry lying close behind the sharp crest and appearing as if held in place by atmospheric pressure, was inaccessible to artillery. There was no place but the bottom of the notch, and that was barely wide enough for the roadbed. From the Confederate side this point was commanded by two batteries posted on a slightly lower elevation beyond a creek, and a half-mile away. All the guns but one were masked by the trees of an orchard; that one—it seemed a bit of impudence—was on an open lawn directly in front of a rather grandiose building, the planter's dwelling. The gun was safe enough in its exposure—but only because the Federal infantry had been forbidden to fire. Coulter's Notch—it came to be called so—was not, that pleasant summer afternoon, a place where one would 'like to put a gun.'

Three or four dead horses lay there sprawling in the road, three or four dead men in a trim row at one side of it, and a little back, down the hill. All but one were cavalrymen belonging to the Federal advance. One was a quartermaster. The general commanding the division and the colonel commanding the brigade, with their staffs and escorts, had ridden into the notch to have a look at the enemy's guns—which had straightway obscured themselves in towering clouds of smoke. It was hardly profitable to be curious about guns which had the trick of the cuttlefish, and the season of observation had been brief. At its conclusion—a short remove backward from where it began—occurred the conversation already partly reported. 'It is the only place,' the general repeated thoughtfully, 'to get at them.'

The colonel looked at him gravely. 'There is room for only one gun, General—one against twelve.'

'That is true—for only one at a time,' said the commander with something like, yet not altogether like, a smile. 'But then, your brave Coulter—a whole battery in himself.'

The tone of irony was now unmistakable. It angered the colonel, but he did not know what to say. The spirit of military subordination is not favourable to retort, nor even to deprecation.

At this moment a young officer of artillery came riding slowly up the road attended by his bugler. It was Captain Coulter. He could not have been more than twenty-three years of age. He was of medium height, but very slender and lithe, and sat his horse with something of the air of a civilian. In face he was of a type singularly unlike the men about him; thin, high-nosed, grey-eyed, with a slight blond moustache, and long, rather straggling hair of the same colour. There was an apparent negligence in his attire. His cap was worn with the visor a trifle askew; his coat was buttoned only at the sword-belt, showing a considerable expanse of white shirt, tolerably clean for that stage of the campaign. But the negligence was all in his dress and bearing; in his face was a look of intense interest in his surroundings. His grey eyes, which seemed occasionally to strike right and left across the landscape, like searchlights, were for the most part fixed upon the sky beyond the Notch; until he should arrive at the summit of the road there was nothing else in that direction to see. As he came opposite his division and brigade commanders at the roadside he saluted mechanically and was about to pass on. The colonel signed to him to halt.

'Captain Coulter,' he said, 'the enemy has twelve pieces over there on the next ridge. If I rightly understand the general, he directs that you bring up a gun and engage them.'

There was a blank silence; the general looked stolidly at a distant regiment swarming slowly up the hill through rough undergrowth, like a torn and draggled cloud of blue smoke; the captain appeared not to have observed him. Presently the captain spoke, slowly and with apparent effort:

'On the next ridge, did you say, sir? Are the guns near the house?'

'Ah, you have been over this road before. Directly at the house.'

'And it is—necessary—to engage them? The order is imperative?'

His voice was husky and broken. He was visibly paler. The colonel was astonished and mortified. He stole a glance at the commander. In that set, immobile face was no sign; it was as hard as bronze. A moment later the general rode away, followed by his staff and escort. The colonel, humiliated and indignant, was about to order Captain Coulter in arrest, when the latter spoke a few words in a low tone to his bugler, saluted, and rode straight forward into the Notch, where, presently, at the summit of the road, his field-glass at his eyes, he showed against the sky, he and his horse, sharply defined and statuesque. The bugler had dashed down the speed and disappeared behind a wood. Presently his bugle was heard singing in the cedars, and in an incredibly short time a single gun with its caisson, each drawn by six horses and manned by its full complement of gunners, came bounding and banging up the grade in a storm of dust, unlimbered under cover, and was run forward by hand to the fatal crest among the dead horses. A gesture of the captain's arm, some strangely agile movements of the men in loading, and almost before the troops along the way had ceased to hear the rattle of the wheels, a great white cloud sprang forward down the slope, and with a deafening report the affair at Coulter's Notch had begun.

It is not intended to relate in detail the progress and incidents of that ghastly contest—a contest without vicissitudes, its alternations only different degrees of despair. Almost at the instant when Captain Coulter's gun blew its challenging cloud twelve answering clouds rolled upward from among the trees about the plantation house, a deep multiple report roared back like a broken echo, and thenceforth to the end the Federal cannoneers fought their hopeless battle in an atmosphere of living iron whose thoughts were lightnings and whose deeds were death.

Unwilling to see the efforts which he could not aid and the slaughter which he could not stay, the colonel ascended the ridge at a point a quarter of a mile to the left, whence the Notch, itself invisible, but pushing up successive masses of smoke, seemed the crater of a volcano in thundering eruption. With his glass he watched the enemy's guns, noting as he could the effects of Coulter's fire—if Coulter still lived to direct it. He saw that the Federal gunners, ignoring those of the enemy's pieces whose positions could be determined by their smoke only, gave their whole attention to the one that maintained its place in the open— the lawn in front of the house. Over and about that hardy piece the shells exploded at intervals of a few seconds. Some exploded in the house, as could be seen by thin ascensions of smoke from the breached roof. Figures of prostrate men and horses were plainly visible.

'If our fellows are doing so good work with a single gun,' said the colonel to an aide who happened to be nearest, 'they must be suffering like the devil from twelve. Go down and present the commander of that piece with my congratulations on the accuracy of his fire.'

Turning to his adjutant-general he said, 'Did you observe Coulter's damned reluctance to obey orders?'

'Yes, sir, I did.'

'Well, say nothing about it, please. I don't think the general will care to make any accusations. He will probably have enough to do in explaining his own connection with this uncommon way of amusing the rearguard of a retreating enemy.'

A young officer approached from below, climbing breathless up the acclivity. Almost before he had saluted, he gasped out:

'Colonel, I am directed by Colonel Harmon to say that the enemy's guns are within easy reach of our rifles, and most of them visible from several points along the ridge.'

The brigade commander looked at him without a trace of interest in his expression. 'I know it,' he said quietly.

The young adjutant was visibly embarrassed. 'Colonel Harmon would like to have permission to silence those guns,' he stammered.

'So should I,' the colonel said in the same tone. 'Present my compliments to Colonel Harmon and say to him that the general's orders for the infantry not to fire are still in force.'

The adjutant saluted and retired. The colonel ground his heel into the earth and turned to look again at the enemy's guns.

'Colonel,' said the adjutant-general, 'I don't know that I ought to say anything, but there is something wrong in all this. Do you happen to know that Captain Coulter is from the South?'

'No, *was* he indeed?'

'I heard that last summer the division which the general then commanded was in the vicinity of Coulter's home—camped there for weeks, and—'

'Listen!' said the colonel, interrupting with an upward gesture. 'Do you hear *that*?'

'That' was the silence of the Federal gun. The staff, the order-lies, the lines of infantry behind the crest—all had 'heard', and were looking curiously in the direction of the crater, whence no smoke now ascended except desultory cloudlets from the enemy's shells. Then came the blare of a bugle, a faint rattle of wheels; a minute later the sharp reports recommenced with double activity. The demolished gun had been replaced with a sound one.

'Yes,' said the adjutant-general, resuming his narrative, 'the general made the acquaintance of Coulter's family. There was trouble—I don't know the exact nature of it—something about Coulter's wife. She is a red-hot Secessionist, as they all are, except Coulter himself, but she is a good wife and a high-bred lady. There was a complaint to army headquarters. The general was trans-ferred to this division. It is odd that Coulter's battery should afterward have been assigned to it.'

'See here, Morrison,' said he, looking his gossiping staff officer straight in the face, 'did you get that story from a gentleman or a liar?'

'I don't want to say how I got it, Colonel, unless it is necessary'—he was blushing a trifle—'but I'll stake my life upon its truth in the main.'

The colonel turned toward a small knot of officers some dis-tance away. 'Lieutenant Williams!' he shouted.

One of the officers detached himself from the group and coming forward, saying: 'Pardon me, Colonel, I thought you had been informed. Williams is dead down there by the gun. What can I do, sir?'

Lieutenant Williams was the aide who had had the pleasure of conveying to the officer in charge of the gun his brigade com-mander's congratulations.

'Go,' said the colonel, 'and direct the withdrawal of that gun instantly. No—I'll go myself.'

He strode down the declivity toward the rear of the Notch at a breakneck pace, over rocks and through brambles, followed by his little retinue in tumultuous disorder. At the foot of the declivity they mounted their waiting animals and took to the road at a lively trot, round a bend and into the Notch. The spectacle which they encountered there was appalling!

Within that defile, barely broad enough for a single gun, were piled the wrecks of no fewer than four. They had noted the silencing of only the last one disabled—there had been a lack of men to replace it quickly with another. The débris lay on both sides of the road; the men had managed to keep an open way between, through which the fifth piece was now firing. The men?—they looked like demons of the pit! All were hatless, all stripped to the waist, their reeking skins black with blotches of powder and spattered with gouts of blood. They worked like madmen, with rammer and cartridge, lever and lanyard. They set their swollen shoulders and bleeding hands against the wheels at each recoil and heaved the heavy gun back to its place. There were no commands; in that awful environment of whooping shot, exploding shells, shrieking fragments of iron, and flying splinters of wood, none could have been heard. Officers, if officers there were, were indistinguishable; all worked together—each while he lasted—governed by the eye. When the gun was sponged, it was loaded; when loaded, aimed and fired. The colonel observed something new to his military experience—something horrible and unnatural: the gun was bleeding at the mouth! In temporary default of water, the man sponging had dipped his sponge into a pool of comrade's blood. In all this work there was no clashing; the duty of the instant was obvious. When one fell, another looking a trifle cleaner, seemed to rise from the earth in the dead man's tracks, to fall in his turn.

With the ruined guns lay the ruined men—alongside the wreckage, under it and atop of it; and back down the road—a ghastly procession!—crept on hands and knees such of the wounded as were able to move. The colonel—he had compassionately sent his cavalcade to the right about—had to ride over those who were entirely dead in order not to crush those who were partly alive. Into that hell he tranquilly held his way, rode up alongside the gun, and, in the obscurity of the last discharge, tapped upon the cheek the man holding the rammer—who straightway fell, thinking himself killed. A fiend seven times damned sprang out of the smoke to take his place, but paused and gazed up at the mounted officer with an unearthly regard, his teeth flashing between his black lips, his eyes, fierce and expanded, burning like coals beneath his bloody brow. The colonel made an authoritative gesture and pointed to the rear. The fiend bowed in token of obedience. It was Captain Coulter.

Simultaneously with the colonel's arresting sign, silence fell upon the whole field of action. The procession of missiles no longer streamed into that defile of death, for the enemy also had ceased firing. His army had been gone for hours, and the commander of his rear-guard, who had held his position perilously long in hope to silence the Federal fire, at that strange moment had silenced his own. 'I was not aware of the breadth of my authority,' said the colonel to anybody, riding forward to the crest to see what had really happened.

An hour later his brigade was in bivouac on the enemy's ground, and its idlers were examining, with something of awe, as the faithful inspect a saint's relics, a score of straddling dead horses and three disabled guns, all spiked. The fallen men had been carried away; their torn and broken bodies would have given too great satisfaction.

Naturally, the colonel established himself and his military family in the plantation house. It was somewhat shattered, but it was better than the open air. The furniture was greatly deranged and broken. Walls and ceilings were knocked away here and there, and a lingering odour of powder smoke was everywhere. The beds, the closets of women's clothing, the cupboards were not greatly damaged. The new tenants for a night made themselves comfortable, and the virtual effacement of Coulter's battery supplied them with an interesting topic.

During supper an orderly of the escort showed himself into the dining-room and asked permission to speak to the colonel.

'What is it, Barbour?' said that officer pleasantly, having overheard the request.

'Colonel, there is something wrong in the cellar; I don't know what—somebody there. I was down there rummaging about.'

'I will go down and see,' said a staff officer, rising.

'So will I,' the colonel said; 'let the others remain. Lead on, orderly.'

They took a candle from the table and descended the cellar stairs, the orderly in visible trepidation. The candle made but a feeble light, but presently, as they advanced, its narrow circle of illumination revealed a human figure seated on the ground against the black stone wall which they were skirting, its knees elevated, its head bowed sharply forward. The face, which should have been seen in profile, was invisible, for the man was bent so far forward that his long hair concealed it; and, strange to relate, the beard, of a much darker hue, fell in a great tangled mass and lay along the ground at his side. They involuntarily paused; then the colonel, taking the candle from the orderly's shaking hand, approached the man and attentively considered him. The long dark beard was the hair of a woman—dead. The dead woman clasped in her arms a dead babe. Both were clasped in the arms of the man, pressed against his breast, against his lips. There was blood in the hair of the woman; there was blood in the hair of the man. A yard away, near an irregular depression in the beaten earth which formed the cellar's floor—a fresh excavation with a convex bit of iron, having jagged edges, visible in one of the sides—lay an infant's foot. The colonel held the light as high as he could. The floor of the room above was broken through, the splinters pointing at all angles downward. 'This casemate is not bomb-proof,' said the colonel gravely. It did not occur to him that his summing up of the matter had any levity in it.

They stood about the group awhile in silence; the staff officer was thinking of his unfinished supper, the orderly of what might possibly be in one of the casks on the other side of the cellar. Suddenly the man whom they had thought dead raised his head and gazed tranquilly into their faces. His complexion was coal black; the cheeks were apparently tattooed in irregular sinuous lines from the eyes downward. The lips, too, were white, like those of a stage Negro. There was blood upon his forehead.

The staff officer drew back a pace, the orderly two paces.

'What are you doing here, my man?' said the colonel, unmoved.

'This house belongs to me, sir,' was the reply, civilly delivered.

'To you? Ah, I see! And these?'

'My wife and child. I am Captain Coulter.'

The Spoils of War

He had been with Wellington for six years now: India, then Portugal and Spain — and now Belgium. But yesterday's battle had been the most appalling of them all. God, he was tired. He had worked all night by lamplight: amputating limbs shattered by round shot; extracting musket and carbine balls from case shot; stitching up sabre wounds. He never ceased to wonder at man's ingenuity to cause destruction among his fellow men in such pitched battles as these. Round shot, a solid sphere of iron about 3 or 4 inches in diameter, which ploughed its way through columns of men and could travel up to a mile on dry ground, was one thing, but he detested case shot or cannister, a thin tin cylinder filled with nearly a hundred musket or carbine balls. These were diabolical, spraying death and mutilation in all directions when discharged. And he never failed to wonder at the grim irony of it all — he was trained to save men's lives, but the generals were dedicated to taking them. Yet he was an army officer, too.

The boy brought him a welcome cup of hot coffee. He took it gratefully without a word. As he sipped it, he looked out across the open ground that had separated the two armies the day before. Here, up on the heights that ran between the ravine at Merbe Braine to the west, and the little hamlet of Ter La Haye to the east, there was a fine view across the plain to the heights to the south nearly a mile away where Napoleon's army had gathered, all around La Belle Alliance. Before the battle the open ground had been under rye almost as tall as a man, but after the infantry and cavalry charges backwards and forwards across it, the rye had been flattened, and now the whole plain looked like something out of a painting by Hieronymous Bosch. The smashed cannons, the dead and dying horses, the innumerable numbers of dead and dying men, their gorgeous and flamboyant uniforms now all reduced to the same drab colour by the rain and the mud. Wellington had already sent out officers to make a rough estimate of casualties. In the space of some six square miles, the officers had estimated about 50,000 dead and wounded; some 20,000 British and Allies, the rest French. The surgeon found these numbers almost incomprehensible.

He continued to look out over the plain, lost in reverie. In his mind he could still see the incredible attack of the French cavalry and lancers, Horse Grenadiers and dragoons, cuirassiers and carabineers. A monstrous avalanche of death that had come towards the heights at a steady pace, grim and determined. The enormous black sea of cavalry had come closer and closer, and the surgeon had felt sure that they were all doomed: nothing could stop such a mass of men and horses. And then he had realized that Wellington and his aides-de-camp were close by, and Wellington was watching the approach quite impassively. He had not given the order to fire to the gunners until the French were only 60 yards away. The effect had been devastating. The whole of the front line of horses went down, like grass before a scythe. The horses behind them could not stop, and piled into them. Chaos reigned at once. Men and horses fell and those behind them could not stop, collided with them, and fell in their turn. The British guns kept up an appalling hail of round shot and cannister; the French casualties were terrible. Then the Household Brigade went in with a will. God knows how many Frenchmen died in that charge. The surgeon had even seen Frenchmen attacking Frenchmen as they tried desperately to retreat from the rain of death from the British guns, hacking their way through their own cavalry to get away from the front to the rear. He had stood rooted to the spot as he watched this unbelievable carnage, until recalled to his duty by the boy.

The surgeon had lost all sense of time during that fearful afternoon. But later — someone said it was about 6.30 p.m. — the Prussians finally erupted on the French right flank. That was the beginning of the end. Napoleon had made one last desperate bid to clear the British and the Allies from the ridge. The surgeon by that time had been working automatically. He had been on his feet all day, and had eaten nothing since noon. A young British dragoon had been brought in with a French musket ball in his back. He had been lucky — it was buried in muscle and had not pierced any vital organ. As the surgeon dressed the wound after extracting the ball, the officer had told him about the final phase of the battle.

Napoleon had finally brought in the Old Guard, his elite troops which had never been beaten throughout the Peninsular War.

Some 4,000 of the Middle Guard made up the first wave; the Old Guard came in the second; and the 2nd and 3rd Grenadiers had acted as a firm base in the valley below. And the incredible had happened. The Imperial Guard had failed. For the first time they had been stopped in their tracks and then routed. Caught between the British and the Allies under Wellington and the Prussians under Blücher, the French had been massacred. No one knew where Napoleon was, but everyone felt sure he had made good his escape, protected by his own personal bodyguard of Imperial Guardsmen.

When the battle had been finally over, and the French were in full rout, the surgeon had gone to the top of the ridge to see the final skirmishings. It had been fine moonlight.

He finished the coffee, and then was suddenly aware that several riders had stopped near him. It was Wellington with a number of senior officers. The Duke came closer and stopped in front of him.

'Well, we did it, John,' he said with a grim smile.

'Yes, Your Grace,' answered the surgeon.

'I just dropped by to remind you of the small commission you promised to do for me at the Duchess of Richmond's ball,' continued the Duke, trying to quieten his restive horse.

My God, the Duchess of Richmond's ball! It seemed a lifetime ago, but it had been only a few days before, at the Rue de la Blanchisserie — 'The Wash-house', as the Duke called her Ladyship's residence in Brussels.

'I had not forgotten, Your Grace,' the surgeon replied. The Duke grunted and wheeled away to the right followed by his escort.

He stood up wearily and, signalling to the boy to follow him, descended the slope to the low-lying ground below and began to walk among the dead and dying, his companion following at a respectful distance. A strange lad. A camp-follower the army had picked up somewhere along the line. In one way, the boy owed him his life. If the surgeon had not chanced by, the soldiers who had found the boy stealing food would have shot him. When in doubt, shoot them: they may be spies! The average foot-soldier was a simple soul, who thought simple thoughts. The boy had been grateful for the surgeon's intervention, of course, and had somehow attached himself to him as a general dogsbody. He was not sorry; there was always so much to be done: teeth to be pulled, wounds to be tended, words of comfort for some poor soul dying hundreds of miles from his English village. He was glad of the boy's company, too.

But the surgeon had learned little of the boy's background. He had told him that his mother had been French but his father an English sailor. Both were dead. Or so he claimed. It made him something of a misfit in this mad and terrible war. He spoke English and French equally well, though roughly. But he had been useful, of that there was no doubt. He had soon ingratiated himself with the officers, acting as an interpreter when French prisoners were questioned. But the common troops did not like him. The fact that he spoke French made them distrust him, so he stuck close to the surgeon who had saved his life.

'Come on, we've work to do.' With that the boy had taken the bag from him and, keeping close to his heels, followed him as he picked his way carefully among the dead and dying.

The surgeon stopped by the body of a young cornet, whose face seemed strangely at peace in the rays of the early morning sun. The surgeon opened the mouth and examined the teeth.

'Here are some good ones — give me the small key.'

The boy took the box of dental keys out of the bag and opened it. The keys looked curiously beautiful nestling in the velvet-lined compartments of the box, their polished brass glinting in the light. The boy took out the smallest and passed it to the surgeon. Expertly, the surgeon extracted two teeth — two upper front incisors. He held them close to his face and inspected them minutely.

'These will do fine.'

He wrapped them carefully in a piece of cloth and gave the small packet to the boy, who placed it equally carefully in the bag.

'Come on, we need a few good back teeth for this job. I don't want to spend all day on this — there are men still alive who need attention.'

They began to pick their way among the bodies again, the surgeon stopping every now and then to open a mouth and inspect the teeth. A little way off, orderlies were attending to wounded English soldiers, and further away, to the left, two foot-soldiers were quarrelling over loot.

The surgeon's face was expressionless, and the boy could not know how the surgeon resented this unpleasant task. It was one thing to pull teeth from the mouths of the living, but quite another to pull teeth from the mouths of the dead. But he had no choice. The Duke of Wellington and the other officers wore out their dead men's teeth so fast, grinding them away so quickly, that the surgeon was always having to replace them. The surgeon had thought so much about artificial teeth, but he never seemed to have the time to devote to the experiments that would be necessary. He had thought for a long time that there must be some material which was so strong and hard that it would last. Once real teeth were dead, they discoloured and became so weak. He sighed. Maybe, when he was retired and out of the army on his pension, he would have the time to experiment. Men couldn't go on using real teeth from dead men for ever — there had to be a better way.

His day-dream was interrupted by a cry from the boy. He looked up and saw that the boy was kneeling by the body of a young French cavalry officer. He was inspecting the teeth.

'These are beautiful teeth, sir,' the boy said respectfully. The surgeon looked at them.

'Yes, they are fine — not a mark on them. I'll take two from these.'

The boy handed him a key — a larger one this time — and the surgeon began his work. As he started to exert pressure on the tooth the young Frenchman suddenly groaned.

'He's still alive, sir,' the boy said quietly. The young cavalry-man opened his eyes and tried to focus them on the surgeon's face.

'De l'eau, de l'eau, pour l'amour de Dieu,' he whispered faintly.

'He's asking for water, sir,' said the boy.

The surgeon took his canteen from his belt and offered it to the boy.

'Here, he can have some of this.'

The boy knelt down and lifted up the Frenchman's head very gently, cradling it in his arms. He raised the canteen to the cavalry-man's swollen lips and the Frenchman drank a little. He smiled weakly at the boy, who continued to support his head. The water made him cough, and a little blood ran down his chin onto his breast-plate. The surgeon saw, for the first time, that the Frenchman had been run through by a lance, very low down on the left side, just above the sash. It was a frightful wound, and the surgeon marvelled that the man was still alive. The Frenchman must have lain wounded for at least fifteen or sixteen hours.

The boy wiped the blood from the dying man's face with great gentleness. Suddenly, the Frenchman's eyes went wide, and he grasped the boy's right arm with both hands.

'Dites-moi, avons-nous gagnée la bataille?'

The boy hesitated only for a moment. Throwing a quick look towards the surgeon, he answered.

'Oui, nous avons gagnée.'

The young Frenchman suddenly relaxed his grip, and a smile of extraordinary serenity appeared on his face. He sighed a little and died in the boy's arms.

'What did he say?' the surgeon asked. The boy looked away across the battle-field.

'He asked if we had won. I don't think he saw you properly. He thought I was French,' replied the boy.

'You said that "we" had, didn't you? At least I know what "yes" is in French!' said the surgeon.

The boy looked uncomfortable for a moment. Then he squared his shoulders, turning towards the surgeon.

'Yes, I did.'

'Good,' said the surgeon. 'At least one poor devil has died content on this God-forsaken soil.'

He stood brooding for a moment, looking out across the plain at the foot-hills in the distance.

'Come on. We've still those damned teeth to get.'

He picked up the bag before the boy could reach it and strode off towards a group of bodies around a cannon. The boy followed without saying anything.

The surgeon walked with a lighter step than before. Perhaps the boy was really French after all. What did it matter, now that Napoleon was finished? Even the thought of having to pull a few more dead men's teeth did not seem so repugnant as before.

The Last Galley

It was a spring morning, one hundred and forty-six years before the coming of Christ. The North African Coast, with its broad hem of golden sand, its green belt of feathery palm trees, and its background of barren, red-scarped hills, shimmered like a dream country in the opal light. Save for a narrow edge of snow-white surf, the Mediterranean lay blue and serene as far as the eye could reach. In all its vast expanse there was no break but for a single galley, which was slowly making its way from the direction of Sicily and heading for the distant harbour of Carthage.

Seen from afar it was a stately and beautiful vessel, deep red in colour, double-banked with scarlet oars, its broad, flapping sail stained with Tyrian purple, its bulwarks gleaming with brass work. A brazen, three-pronged ram projected in front, and a high golden figure of Baal, the God of the Phoenicians, children of Canaan, shone upon the afterdeck. From the single high mast above the huge sail streamed the tiger-striped flag of Carthage. So, like some stately scarlet bird, with golden beak and wings of purple, she swam upon the face of the waters—a thing of might and of beauty as seen from the distant shore.

But approach and look at her now! What are these dark streaks which foul her white decks and dapple her brazen shields? Why do the long red oars move out of time, irregular, convulsive? Why are some missing from the staring portholes, some snapped with jagged, yellow edges, some trailing inert against the side? Why are two prongs of the brazen ram twisted and broken? See, even the high image of Baal is battered and disfigured! By every sign this ship has passed through some grievous trial, some day of terror, which has left its heavy marks upon her.

And now stand upon the deck itself, and see more closely the men who man her! There are two decks forward and aft, while in the open waist are the double banks of seats, above and below, where the rowers, two to an oar, tug and bend at their endless task. Down the centre is a narrow platform, along which pace a line of warders, lash in hand, who cut cruelly at the slave who pauses, be it only for an instant, to sweep the sweat from his dripping brow. But these slaves—look at them! Some are captured Romans, some Sicilians, many black Libyans, but all are in the last exhaustion, their weary eyelids drooped over their eyes, their lips thick with black crusts, and pink with bloody froth, their arms and backs moving mechanically to the hoarse chant of the overseer. Their bodies, of all tints from ivory to jet, are stripped to the waist, and every glistening back shows the angry stripes of the warders. But it is not from these that the blood comes which reddens the seats and tints the salt water washing beneath their manacled feet. Great gaping wounds, the marks of sword slash and spear stab, show crimson upon their naked chests and shoulders, while many lie huddled and senseless athwart the benches, careless for ever of the whips which still hiss above them. Now we can understand those empty portholes and those trailing oars.

Nor were the crew in better case than their slaves. The decks were littered with wounded and dying men. It was but a remnant who still remained upon their feet. The most lay exhausted upon the foredeck, while a few of the more zealous were mending their shattered armour, restringing their bows, or cleaning the deck from the marks of combat. Upon a raised platform at the base of the mast stood the sailing-master, who conned the ship, his eyes fixed upon the distant point of Megara which screened the eastern side of the Bay of Carthage. On the afterdeck were gathered a number of officers, silent and brooding, glancing from time to time at two of their own class who stood apart deep in conversation. The one, tall, dark, and wiry, with pure, Semitic features, and the limbs of a giant, was Magro, the famous Carthaginian captain, whose name was still a terror on every shore, from Gaul to the Euxine. The other, a white-bearded, swarthy man, with indomitable courage and energy stamped upon every eager line of his keen, aquiline face, was Gisco the politician, a man of the highest Punic blood, a Suffete of the purple robe, and the leader of that party in the State which had watched and striven amid the selfishness and slothfulness of his fellow-countrymen to rouse the public spirit and waken the public conscience to the ever-increasing danger from Rome. As they talked, the two men glanced continually, with earnest anxious faces, towards the northern skyline.

'It is certain,' said the older man, with gloom in his voice and bearing, 'none have escaped save ourselves.'

'I did not leave the press of the battle while I saw one ship which I could succour,' Magro answered. 'As it was, we came away, as you saw, like a wolf which has a hound hanging on to either haunch. The Roman dogs can show the wolf-bites which prove it. Had any other galley won clear, they would surely be with us by now, since they have no place of safety save Carthage.'

The younger warrior glanced keenly ahead to the distant point which marked his native city. Already the low, leafy hill could be seen, dotted with the white villas of the wealthy Phoenician merchants. Above them, a gleaming dot against the pale blue morning sky, shone the brazen roof of the citadel of Byrsa, which capped the sloping town.

'Already they can see us from the watch-towers,' he remarked. 'Even from afar they may know the galley of Black Magro. But which of all of them will guess that we alone remain of all that goodly fleet which sailed out with blare of trumpet and roll of drum but one short month ago?'

The patrician smiled bitterly. 'If it were not for our great ancestors and for our beloved country, the Queen of the Waters,' said he, 'I could find it in my heart to be glad at this destruction which has come upon this vain and feeble generation. You have spent your life upon the seas, Magro. You do not know how it has been with us on the land. But I have seen this canker grow upon us which now leads us to our death. I and others have gone down into the market-place to plead with the people, and been pelted with mud for our pains. Many a time have I pointed to Rome, and said, "Behold these people, who bear arms themselves, each man for his own duty and pride. How can you who hide behind mercenaries hope to stand against them?"—a hundred times I have said it.'

'And had they no answer?' asked the Rover.

'Rome was far off and they could not see it, so to them it was nothing,' the old man answered. 'Some thought of trade, and some of votes, and some of profits from the State, but none would see that the State itself, the mother of all things, was sinking to her end. So might the bees debate who should have wax or honey when the torch was blazing which would bring to ashes the hive and all therein. "Are we not rulers of the sea?" "Was not Hannibal a great man?" Such were their cries, living ever in the past and blind to the future. Before that sun sets there will be tearing of hair and rending of garments; but what will that now avail us?'

'It is some sad comfort,' said Magro, 'to know that what Rome holds she cannot keep.'

'Why say you that? When we go down, she is supreme in all the world.'

'For a time, and only for a time,' Magro answered gravely. 'Yet you will smile, perchance, when I tell you how it is that I know it. There was a wise woman who lived in that part of the Tin Islands which juts forth into the sea, and from her lips I have heard many things, but not one which has not come aright. Of the fall of our own country, and even of this battle, from which we now return, she told me clearly. There is much strange lore amongst these savage peoples in the west of the land of Tin.'

'What said she of Rome?'

'That she also would fall, even as we, weakened by her riches and her factions.'

Gisco rubbed his hands. 'That at least makes our own fall less bitter,' said he. 'But since we have fallen, and Rome will fall, who in turn may hope to be Queen of the Waters?'

'That also I asked her,' said Magro, 'and gave her my Tyrian belt with the golden buckle as a guerdon for her answer. But, indeed, it was too high payment for the tale she told, which must be false if all else she said was true. She would have it that in coming days it was her own land, this fog-girt isle where painted savages can scarce row a wicker coracle from point to point, which shall at last take the trident which Carthage and Rome have dropped.'

The smile which flickered upon the old patrician's keen features died away suddenly, and his fingers closed upon his companion's wrist. The other hand set rigid, his head advanced, his hawk eyes upon the northern skyline. Its straight, blue horizon was broken by two low black dots.

'Galleys!' whispered Gisco.

The whole crew had seen them. They clustered along the starboard bulwarks, pointing and chattering. For a moment the gloom of defeat was lifted, and a buzz of joy ran from group to group at the thought that they were not alone—that some one had escaped the great carnage as well as themselves.

'By the spirit of Baal,' said Black Magro, 'I could not have believed that any could have fought clear from such a welter. Could it be young Hamilcar in the *Africa*, or is it Beneva in the blue Syrian ship? We three with others may form a squadron and make head against them yet. If we hold our course, they will join us ere we round the harbour mole.'

Slowly the injured galley toiled on her way, and more swiftly the two newcomers swept down from the north. Only a few miles off lay the green point and the white houses which flanked the great African city. Already, upon the headland, could be seen a dark group of waiting townsmen. Gisco and Magro were still watching with puckered gaze the approaching galleys, when the brown Libyan boatswain, with flashing teeth and gleaming eyes, rushed upon the poop, his long thin arm stabbing to the north.

'Romans!' he cried. 'Romans!'

A hush had fallen over the great vessel. Only the wash of the water and the measured rattle and beat of the oars broke in upon the silence.

'By the horns of God's altar, I believe the fellow is right!' cried old Gisco. 'See how they swoop upon us like falcons. They are full-manned and full-oared.'

'Plain wood, unpainted,' said Magro. 'See how it gleams yellow where the sun strikes it.'

'And yonder thing beneath the mast. Is it not the cursed bridge they use for boarding?'

'So they grudge us even one,' said Magro with a bitter laugh. 'Not even one galley shall return to the old sea-mother. Well, for my part, I would as soon have it so. I am of a mind to stop the oars and await them.'

'It is a man's thought,' answered old Gisco; 'but the city will need us in the days to come. What shall it profit us to make the Roman victory complete? Nay, Magro, let the slaves row as they never rowed before, not for our own safety, but for the profit of the State.'

So the great red ship laboured and lurched onwards, like a weary panting stag which seeks shelter from his pursuers, while ever swifter and ever nearer sped the two lean fierce galleys from the north. Already the morning sun shone upon the lines of low Roman helmets above the bulwarks, and glistened on the silver wave where each sharp prow shot through the still blue water. Every moment the ships drew nearer, and the long thin scream of the Roman trumpets grew louder upon the ear.

Upon the high bluff of Megara there stood a great concourse of the people of Carthage who had hurried forth from the city upon the news that the galleys were in sight. They stood now, rich and poor, effete and plebeian, white Phoenician and dark Kabyle, gazing with breathless interest at the spectacle before them. Some hundreds of feet beneath them the Punic galley had drawn so close that with their naked eyes they could see those stains of battle which told their dismal tale. The Romans, too, were heading in such a way that it was before their very faces that their ship was about to be cut off; and yet of all this multitude not one could raise a hand in its defence. Some wept in impotent grief, some cursed with flashing eyes and knotted fists, some on their knees held up appealing hands to Baal; but neither prayer, tears, nor curses could undo the past nor mend the present. That broken, crawling galley meant that their fleet was gone. Those two fierce darting ships meant that the hands of Rome were already at their throat. Behind them would come others and others, the innumerable trained hosts of the great Republic, long mistress of the land, now dominant also upon the waters. In a month, two months, three at the most, their armies would be there, and what could all the untrained multitudes of Carthage do to stop them?

'Nay!' cried one, more hopeful than the rest, 'at least we are brave men with arms in our hands.'

'Fool!' said another, 'is it not such talk which has brought us to our ruin? What is the brave man untrained to the brave man trained? When you stand before the sweep and rush of a Roman legion you may learn the difference.'

'Then let us train!'

'Too late! A full year is needful to turn a man to a soldier. Where will you—where will your city be within the year? Nay, there is but one chance for us. If we give up our commerce and our colonies, if we strip ourselves of all that made us great, then perchance the Roman conqueror may hold his hand.'

And already the last sea-fight of Carthage was coming swiftly to an end before them. Under their very eyes the two Roman galleys had shot in, one on either side of the vessel of Black Magro. They had grappled with him, and he, desperate in his despair, had cast the crooked flukes of his anchors over their gunwales, and bound them to him in an iron grip, whilst with hammer and crowbar he burst great holes in his own sheathing. The last Punic galley should never be rowed into Ostia, a sight for the holiday-makers of Rome. She would lie in her own waters. And the fierce, dark soul of her rover captain glowed as he thought that not alone should she sink into the depths of her mother sea.

Too late did the Romans understand the man with whom they had to deal. Their boarders who had flooded the Punic decks felt the planking sink and sway beneath them. They rushed to gain

Acknowledgements

The editor wishes to thank the authors (or their agents or trustees) and publishers who have granted permission to reproduce the following copyright material:

'Intelligence' by C.S. Forester, from *Gold from Crete* (Michael Joseph Ltd). Reprinted by permission of A.D. Peters & Co. Ltd.

'The Young Man from Kalgoorlie' by H.E. Bates, from *The Stories of Flying Officer 'X'* (Jonathan Cape Ltd). Reprinted by permission of the Estate of the late H.E. Bates.

'Monsoon Selection Board' by George Macdonald Fraser (Pan Books).

'Turning Point' by Alan Green. Reprinted by permission of the author.

'Death of the Zulu' by Uys Krige. Reprinted by permission of the Dramatic, Artistic and Literary Rights Organization (Pty) Ltd.

'They Came' by Alun Lewis, from *Last Inspection* (George Allen & Unwin Ltd).

'The Alien Skull' by Liam O'Flaherty, from *The Short Stories of Liam O'Flaherty* (Jonathan Cape Ltd).

'The Spoils of War' by Carey Blyton. Reprinted by permission of the author.

their own vessels; but they, too, were being drawn downwards, held in the dying grip of the great red galley. Over they went and ever over. Now the deck of Magro's ship is flush with the water, and the Romans, drawn towards it by the iron bonds which held them, are tilted downwards, one bulwark upon the waves, one reared high in the air. Madly they strain to cast off the death-grip of the galley. She is under the surface now, and ever swifter, with the greater weight, the Roman ships heel after her. There is a rending crash. The wooden side is torn out of one, and mutilated, dismembered, she rights herself, and lies a helpless thing upon the water. But a last yellow gleam in the blue water shows where her consort has been dragged to her end in the iron death-grapple of her foemen. The tiger-striped flag of Carthage has sunk beneath the swirling surface, never more to be seen upon the face of the sea.

For in that year a great cloud hung for seventeen days over the African coast, a deep black cloud which was the dark shroud of the burning city. And when the seventeen days were over, Roman ploughs were driven from end to end of the charred ashes, and salt was scattered there as a sign that Carthage should be no more. And far off a huddle of naked, starving folk stood upon the distant mountains, and looked down upon the desolate plain which had once been the fairest and richest upon earth. And they understood too late that it is the law of heaven that the world is given to the hardy and to the self-denying, whilst he who would escape the duties of manhood will soon be stripped of the pride, the wealth, and the power, which are the prizes which manhood brings.